THE MORAL DYNAMICS OF ECONOMIC LIFE

THE MORAL DYNAMICS OF ECONOMIC LIFE

An Extension and Critique of *Caritas in veritate*

Edited by Daniel K. Finn

OXFORD
UNIVERSITY PRESS

Oxford University Press, Inc., publishes works that further
Oxford University's objective of excellence
in research, scholarship, and education.

Oxford New York
Auckland Cape Town Dar es Salaam Hong Kong Karachi
Kuala Lumpur Madrid Melbourne Mexico City Nairobi
New Delhi Shanghai Taipei Toronto

With offices in
Argentina Austria Brazil Chile Czech Republic France Greece
Guatemala Hungary Italy Japan Poland Portugal Singapore
South Korea Switzerland Thailand Turkey Ukraine Vietnam

Published by Oxford University Press, Inc.
198 Madison Avenue, New York, New York 10016

www.oup.com

Library of Congress Cataloging-in-Publication Data
The moral dynamics of economic life : an extension and critique of
Caritas in veritate / edited by Daniel K. Finn.
p. cm.
Proceedings of a symposium held Oct. 15–16, 2010 in Rome, Italy.
Includes bibliographical references (p.).
ISBN 978-0-19-985833-0 (hardcover : alk. paper)—ISBN 978-0-19-985835-4
(pbk. : alk. paper)—ISBN 978-0-19-985834-7 (ebook) 1. Catholic Church.
Pope (2005– : Benedict XVI). Caritas in veritate—Congresses.
2. Economics—Religious aspects—Catholic Church—Congresses.
3. Christian sociology—Catholic Church—Congresses.
4. Christian ethics—Catholic authors—Congresses. I. Finn, Daniel K., 1947–
BX1795.E27M67 2012
241′.4—dc23 2011035839

1 3 5 7 9 8 6 4 2

Printed in the United States of America
on acid-free paper

CONTENTS

FOREWORD

Catholic social teaching presses us to reflect on what it means to be authentically human in the light of faith and reason, and in the ceaseless universal quest for the common good. The symposium cosponsored by the Institute of Advanced Catholic Studies and the Pontifical Council for Justice and Peace in October 2010, titled "*Caritas in veritate* and the United States," sought to articulate both the challenges we face as a human family and the hope offered by the sound Christian, indeed human, principles illuminated by Pope Benedict XVI. Clearly, recent global events awaken us to the importance of a sustained Christian reflection on the nature and goal of human development and economic life.

The symposium afforded scholars from the United States and Europe a unique opportunity to gather in Rome to wrestle with *Caritas in veritate* and its identification of the twin call for love and truth in our lives as citizens, entrepreneurs, workers, students, and, most fundamentally, as followers of Christ and subjects of reason. This volume presents a synthesis of the various statements offered by the participants in the symposium. I am grateful to Professor Dan Finn, Paul Caron, and Fr. James Heft, SM, for arranging for this publication.

An encyclical is an ecclesial document, not an economic, financial, or political statement. It is a letter addressed to the Church—to the bishops and Catholic faithful—and to all people of good will. Thus, although *Caritas in veritate* addresses a wide variety of problems in the world today, it does so from a theological, anthropological, moral, and religious point of view, and it must be understood from this perspective. It is here that we find the encyclical's true foundation. Indeed, the theological, moral, and religious point of view of the social doctrine of the Church is a vision that corresponds to knowledge, including both a suprarational revealed knowledge and a rational knowledge produced by human reason.

Catholic social teaching does not have a purely dogmatic nature, even though it is theological and contains some dogmatic truth, for example, that Jesus Christ is the Son of God, that God is a Trinity of persons, and that we humans are created in God's image and likeness. This social teaching contains mostly elements of a moral character, but it is grounded on deeper theological foundations. It is important in this regard to emphasize the claim that *Caritas in veritate* makes, namely, that "in Jesus Christ is the first and principal factor of integral human development" (*CV*, 8).

How then should the expression "human development" be understood? It should not be understood only as economic development. "Integral human development" is the first principle of all morality, natural and supernatural, yet it clearly concerns integral human fulfillment. Great ethicists such as John Finnis have demonstrated this point. *Caritas in veritate* calls for an interdisciplinary approach to development, making a necessary link between the various sciences, such as theology and economics, theology and politics, and theology and philosophy.

It is possible to engage in a dialogue between different fields of knowledge because they are all grounded in human reason, with which all people are endowed by virtue of their creation by God. Human reason can be purified and consolidated within the broader context of trans-disciplinarity offered by revelation, because divine revelation provides a knowledge that is in no way contrary to reason.

The Institute for Advanced Catholic Studies, together with all organizations dedicated to promoting the social doctrine of the Church, can rightly engage in the formation of a new ethic, one that surpasses the constricted ethic inherited from Thomas Hobbes, the ethics of "discontinuity"—as Ronald Dworkin has said—between personal and public ethics. *Caritas in veritate* aims at precisely such a new ethic, one that goes beyond the dichotomy that postmodernity has set up between ethics and truth, ethics and technology, ethics and finance, and ethics and politics. The encyclical endeavors to help us construct not only a new metaphysical vision but an ethic of relation, which will then compel us to be genuinely concerned about the institutions we build. *Caritas in veritate* speaks to this vision, and about the "institutional path of charity," which insists on the public role of Christians in building a just world (*CV*, 5, 7).

In the same way, *Caritas in veritate* also invites us to engender an ethic of virtue (*CV*, 71). Pope Benedict clearly identifies the need for virtuous people to be engaged in business and politics, persons who live according to their convictions with integrity and who, as a result, will work effectively for the common good. But how is it possible to have an ethic of virtue? This ethic can be realized by going beyond the proposition of Hugo Grotius, who conceived of a society *etsi Deus non daretur*, as if God does not exist. To overcome the dichotomies inherent in such a project, the encyclical proposes a new ethic with God as its foundation. Indeed, as the Holy Father teaches, it is only by acknowledging God as the Supreme Truth and the Supreme Good that we can bring unity to the many choices we are called to make, thus enabling us to recognize the hierarchy of goods and values that gives top priority to the spiritual and a proper ordering of material and technical goods. It is only when God is our reference point that we will be able to restore the telos of human ethics and thus offer to human behavior a global vision, the good of all humanity and of every person.

The Pontifical Council for Justice and Peace pursues two essential mandates: (1) the theoretical study of Catholic social teaching, and therefore many of the contemporary social problems facing the Church and the human family; and (2) the diffusion and implementation of Catholic social doctrine. As academicians, practitioners, and people of faith, the participants of the symposium can assist the Pontifical Council for Justice and Peace by exposing not only the positive elements of the thinking of Amartya Sen, Joseph Stiglitz, and John Rawls, but also their limits. They are thinkers of great stature, but although they share some fundamental principles with the social doctrine of the Church, there remain some weaknesses in their theories. Amartya Sen, for example, insists that we must build a new ethics from the point of view of the impartial spectator, that is, from an external, disinterested view of the person and subject of conduct. *Caritas in veritate,* on the other hand, proposes that we construct an ethic from the perspective of the person open to a relationship with God.

Our gathering in Rome to discuss the theme *Caritas in veritate* and the United States allowed the participants to open windows and to examine new aspects of the social question, and this is of great importance to the work of the Pontifical Council. It is my hope that the synthesis that follows will inspire readers to help make known to others that Catholic social teaching is not a well-kept secret but a treasure of the ecclesial community, available to all. It does not belong exclusively to the pope, the bishops, or the Pontifical Council for Justice and Peace, but it is also the prerogative of each local church and a resource for each person.

Our world badly needs authentic human fulfillment and integral development. *Caritas in veritate* suggests a new ethos is possible only if it is motivated by religion, by dialogue with God. Only this can provide a solid foundation upon which to build a life both truly human and destined for a promise that exceeds any earthly fulfillment.

Mario Toso, SDB
Secretary
Pontifical Council for Justice and Peace
January 2012

CONTRIBUTORS

John L. Allen is an American journalist who divides his time between Rome and the United States. He specializes in news about the Catholic Church and is senior correspondent for the *National Catholic Reporter* and senior Vatican analyst for CNN. Allen is the author of several books, including *The Future Church: How Ten Trends Are Revolutionizing the Catholic Church* and *All the Pope's Men: The Inside Story of How the Vatican Really Thinks.* He has also written two biographies of Pope Benedict XVI, the first one published in 2000 when he was still a cardinal, and the first biography of him in English.

Dr. Mary Jo Bane is Thornton Bradshaw Professor of Public Policy and Management and academic dean, John F. Kennedy School of Government, Harvard University. She has served as assistant secretary for children and families at the U.S. Department of Health and Human Services and commissioner of the New York State Department of Social Services. Her publications include *Lifting Up the Poor: A Dialogue on Religion, Poverty, and Welfare Reform* (coauthor), and "The Catholic Puzzle: Parishes and Civic Life" in *Taking Faith Seriously,* and "Voice and Loyalty in the Church: The People of God, Politics and Management" in *Common Calling: The Laity and Governance of the Catholic Church.* She holds a BS from Georgetown University School of Foreign Service; and MA and DEd from Harvard University.

Fr. Albino Barrera, O.P., is professor of economics and theology, Providence College. His publications include *Market Complicity and Christian Ethics; Globalization and Economic Ethics: Distributive Justice in the Knowledge Economy; Economic Compulsion and Christian Ethics; God and the Evil of Scarcity: Moral Foundations of Economic Agency*; and *Modern Catholic Social Documents and Political Economy*. He is a licentiate in theology (STL), the Dominican House of Studies, Washington, DC, and holds a PhD in economics from Yale University.

Dr. Rebecca M. Blank is undersecretary for economic affairs in the U.S. Department of Commerce. Her office produces economic and policy analysis and she oversees the two largest U.S. statistical agencies, the Census Bureau and the Bureau of Economic Analysis. Prior to this, she was dean of the Gerald R. Ford School of Public Policy at the University of Michigan and codirector of the National Poverty Center. She served as a member of President Clinton's Council of Economic Advisers and is a member of the American Academy of Arts and Sciences. She has also taught economics at Northwestern University and Princeton. Her books include *It Takes a Nation: A New Agenda for Fighting Poverty; Is the Market Moral?* (with William McGurn); and *Do Justice: Linking Christian Faith and Modern Economic Life*.

Dr. Luk Bouckaert is emeritus professor of ethics at the Catholic University of Leuven (K.U. Leuven, Belgium). He is a philosopher and an economist by training. His research and publications fall within the fields of business ethics and spirituality. In 1987 he cofounded the interdisciplinary Centre for Economics and Ethics at Leuven. In 2000 he started the SPES Forum (Spirituality in Economics and Society) and some years later the international European SPES Forum. He has written several books in Dutch. Recent publications in English include *Spirituality as a Public Good* (coedited with Laszlo Zsolnai); *Frugality: Rebalancing Material and Spiritual Values in Economic Life* (coedited with H. Opdebeeck and L. Zsolnai); and *Imagine Europe* (coedited with J. Eynikel).

Fr. John A. Coleman, S.J., is recently retired from the Charles Casassa Chair of Social Values at Loyola Marymount University. He has published widely on issues related to the sociology of religion, Catholic social thought, social theory, and theories of justice. He has been a research fellow at the Woodstock Center, the Woodrow Wilson Center for International Scholars, the University of Chicago's Institute for Advanced Studies in Religion, and elsewhere. Publications include *Christian Political Ethics* (editor) and *One Hundred Years of Catholic Social Teaching* (editor). He holds BA, MA, Licentiate in Philosophy degrees from St. Louis University; the STM, Licentiate in Theology, from Santa Clara University; and a PhD in sociology from the University of California, Berkeley.

Miguel H. Diaz is U.S. ambassador to the Holy See and professor of theology at the College of Saint Benedict and Saint John's University, Minnesota (on leave). He is a past president of ACHTUS (the Academy of Catholic Hispanic Theologians in the US) and a past member of the board of the Catholic Theological Society of America and of the Karl Rahner Society. His publications include *On Being Human: U.S. Hispanic and Rahnerian Perspectives* and *From the Heart of Our People: Explorations in Catholic Systematic Theology* (coedited). He holds a BA from St. Thomas University, and MA and PhD from the University of Notre Dame.

Dr. Daniel K. Finn is professor of theology and William E. and Virginia Clemens Professor of Economics and the Liberal Arts, St. John's University, Collegeville, Minnesota. He is a past president of the Catholic Theological Society of America, the Association for Social Economics, and the Society of Christian Ethics. He represents the Institute for Advanced Catholic Studies in a project to engage the Catholic Church in Latin America in work with civil society organizations to confront government corruption. His books include *The Moral Ecology of Markets: Assessing Claims about Markets and Justice* and *The True Wealth of Nations: Catholic Social Thought and Economic Life* (editor). He holds a BS from St. John Fisher College, and MA and PhD from the University of Chicago. He is codirector of the True Wealth of Nations research project.

Fr. J. Bryan Hehir is Parker Gilbert Montgomery Professor of the Practice of Religion and Public Life, Kennedy School of Government, Harvard University, and secretary for health care and social services for the

Archdiocese of Boston. He has also served as dean of Harvard Divinity School and on the staff of the U.S. Conference of Catholic Bishops for nineteen years. His writings include *The Moral Measurement of War: A Tradition of Continuity and Change*; *Military Intervention and National Sovereignty*; *Catholicism and Democracy*; and *Social Values and Public Policy: A Contribution from a Religious Tradition*. He holds a BA and MDiv from St. John's Seminary, and ThD from Harvard Divinity School.

Fr. Kenneth R. Himes, OFM, is associate professor of theology, Boston College. He has served as editor of *New Theology Review*, a fellow of the Center for Theological Inquiry in Princeton, New Jersey, and theological consultant for the Office of Social Development and World Peace at the U.S. Conference of Catholic Bishops. He is the editor of the reference volume *Modern Catholic Social Teaching: Commentaries and Interpretations*. He is a past president of the Catholic Theological Society of America. He holds a BA from Siena College, MA from Washington Theological Union, and PhD from Duke University.

Dr. Mary L. Hirschfeld is assistant professor in the Department of Humanities and Augustinian Traditions at Villanova University. She earned a doctorate in economics at Harvard University and was a professor of economics at Occidental College for fifteen years, specializing in the fields of macroeconomics and economic history, feminist economics, and heterodox approaches to economic theory. Her work has been published in the *Review of Economics and Statistics*, *Journal of Economic Education*, *History of Political Economy*, and *Journal of the Society of Christian Ethics*. After a conversion to Catholicism, she left her position to study theology at Notre Dame. She holds a BA from Washington State, PhD from Harvard, and PhD from Notre Dame.

Fr. David Hollenbach, SJ, holds the University Chair in Human Rights and International Justice and is director of the Center for Human Rights and International Justice at Boston College. He also regularly serves as visiting professor at Hekima College, Catholic University of Eastern Africa, Nairobi, Kenya. He is a past president of the Society of Christian Ethics and serves on a number of academic and other boards. His recent books are *Driven from Home: Protecting the Rights of Forced Migrants* and *Refugee Rights: Ethics Advocacy and Africa*. He holds a BS from St. Joseph's University, Philadelphia; PhL, St. Louis University; MA, St. Louis University; MDiv, Woodstock College; and PhD, Yale University.

Dr. Katherine Marshall is visiting professor in the Department of Government, senior fellow at the Berkley Center for Religion, Peace, and World Affairs, Georgetown University, and executive director of World Faiths Development Dialogue. She has worked for almost four decades on international development, with a focus on issues facing the world's poorest countries. Her long career with the World Bank (1971–2006) involved a wide range of leadership assignments, including a focus on ethics, values, and faith in development work, as counselor to the World Bank's president. She serves on the boards of several NGOs, including the Opus Prize Foundation and Avina Americas. She chairs the international selection committee for the Niwano Peace Prize. She holds a BA from Wellesley College and MPA from Woodrow Wilson School, Princeton University.

Bishop William F. Murphy is bishop of Rockville Centre, New York. He has taught at Pope John XXIII Seminary, Weston, Massachusetts; St. John's Seminary, Brighton, Massachusetts; and Emmanuel College, Boston. He has served as undersecretary of the Pontifical Council for Justice and Peace and has published on the economy and Catholic social teaching. He has served both the Holy See and the U.S. Bishops Conference on a number of committees and assignments and was chairman of the USCCB Committee for Domestic Justice and Human Dignity. He holds an AB from Saint John's Seminary, and STL and STD from Pontifical Gregorian University.

Dr. Michael J. Naughton is the Alan W. Moss Professor in Catholic Social Thought and director of John A. Ryan Institute for Catholic Social Thought at the University of St. Thomas, St. Paul, Minnesota. His books include *Rediscovering Abundance: Interdisciplinary Essays on Wealth, Income and Their Distribution in the Catholic Social Tradition* (coedited); *Managing as if Faith Mattered: Christian Social Principles in the Modern Organization* (coauthored); and *Rethinking the Purpose of Business: Interdisciplinary Essays in the Catholic Social Tradition* (coedited).

He holds a PhD from Marquette University, and an MBA from University of St. Thomas.

Michael Novak holds the George Frederick Jewett Chair in Religion and Public Policy at the American Enterprise Institute, Washington, DC. He has served as ambassador of the U.S. Delegation to the UN Human Rights Commission in Geneva and has received the Templeton Prize for Progress in Religion. He lectures widely and has published many articles and books on Christianity and economic life, including *No One Sees God: The Dark Night of Atheists and Believers* and *The Spirit of Democratic Capitalism.* He holds a BA from Stonehill College, a BA from the Gregorian University, and an MA from Harvard University.

Rev. Paulinus I. Odozor, CSSp, is associate professor of moral theology and the theology of the world Church at the University of Notre Dame and is president of the Governing Council of Spiritan International School of Theology, Enugu, Nigeria, where he was teacher and academic dean from 1993 to 1999. His publications include *Richard A. McCormick and the Renewal of Moral Theology* and *Moral Theology in an Age of Renewal: A Study of the Catholic Tradition since Vatican II.* In addition to his academic engagements, Fr. Odozor has held positions of pastoral leadership in Nigeria, Canada, and the United States. In October 2009 he was invited by Pope Benedict XVI to be a special expert assistant to the Second Special Assembly for Africa of the Synod of Bishops.

Dr. Matthew J. Slaughter is Signal Companies' Professor of Management and associate dean of the MBA Program at the Tuck School of Business at Dartmouth. He is a research associate at the National Bureau of Economic Research and a senior fellow at the Council on Foreign Relations. Professor Slaughter has published dozens of articles as book chapters and in peer-reviewed journals; he has coauthored four books, including *The Squam Lake Report: Fixing the Financial System* and *Globalization and the Perceptions of American Workers.* He holds a BA from University of Notre Dame and a PhD from Massachusetts Institute of Technology.

Bishop Mario Toso is secretary of the Pontifical Council for Justice and Peace and titular bishop of Bisarcio. He earned a doctorate in philosophy from the Pontifical Salesian University in 1981 and a licentiate in theology at the Pontifical Lateran University in 1982. Since 1980, he has served as professor of philosophy at the Pontifical Salesian University and from 1991 as professor of theoretical philosophy. From 1994 to 2000, he served as dean of the faculty of philosophy. In 2003, he was appointed rector, a position he held until 2009. Bishop Toso was one of the collaborators consulted for Pope Benedict XVI's encyclical letter *Caritas in Veritate.*

Cardinal Peter Kodwo Turkson is president of the Pontifical Council for Justice and Peace. Born in Ghana in 1948, he was ordained a priest at age twenty-six and archbishop of Cape Coast, Ghana, at age forty-four. Ten years later he was made a cardinal by Pope John Paul II. He served on the faculty of St. Teresa's Seminary of Amisano and of St. Peter's Regional Seminary in Pedu, and has held many other positions within the Church, both in Africa and in Rome. He remains chairman of the Ghana National Peace Council, is the honorary president of the World Conference of Religions for Peace, and is a member of the Association of Ghana Biblical Exegetes. His published work includes "Inculturation: A Biblical Perspective" and "The Evangelization in Africa." He speaks fluent Fante, English, French, Italian, German, and Hebrew. He holds a licenciate and a doctorate in sacred scripture from the Pontifical Biblical Institute, Rome.

Professor Amelia J. Uelmen is on the faculty of the Georgetown University School of Law. Her scholarship focuses on how Catholic social thought can shed light on tort law, legal ethics, and legal education. She has also worked as a consultant for the Focolare's Economy of Communion project. Her publications include *Education's Highest Aim: Teaching and Learning Through a Spirituality of Communion* (coauthored) and "Religious Lawyering's Second Wave," in *Bench and Bar: Ethics,* Institute of Chartered Financial Analysts of India (coauthor). She holds a BA and JD from Georgetown University, and an MA in theology from Fordham University.

Dr. Johan Verstraeten is professor of theological ethics, coordinator of the Interdisciplinary Centre for Religious Studies and Interreligious Dialogue, and director of the Centre for Catholic Social Thought at the Catholic University of Leuven. He also delivers interactive seminars on leadership and spirituality to senior executives at the Avicenna Academy for Leadership and the Comenius International Leadership Programme (Netherlands). He has published widely on religious ethics, business ethics, leadership, and spirituality, including *Catholic Social Thought: Twilight or Renaissance?* (coauthor), *Scrutinizing the Signs of the Times in the Light of the Gospel* (coauthor), *Business Ethics: Broadening the Perspectives* (editor), and several books in Dutch. From 1996 to 2004 he was director and chairman of the European Ethics Network, and he is a cofounder of the International Association for Catholic Social Thought.

Dr. Stefano Zamagni is professor of economics at the University of Bologna, where he has also served as dean of the faculty of economics and senior adjunct professor of international economics and vice director of the Bologna Center of the Johns Hopkins University. He is a member of the Academy of Sciences, Bologna, Modena, and Milan and a member of several editorial boards. He has long served the Pontifical Academy of Social Science and has been a contributor to the Pontifical Council for Justice and Peace. His books include *Civil Economy: Efficiency, Equity, Public Happiness* (coauthored) and *Cooperative Enterprise: Facing the Challenge of Globalization* (coauthored). He did his studies in economics at the University of Milan and Oxford University.

THE MORAL DYNAMICS OF ECONOMIC LIFE

Introduction

Caritas in veritate is the "social encyclical" of Pope Benedict XVI, following in the footsteps of his predecessors from Leo XIII to John Paul II. Benedict presents both a detailed theological basis for the tradition of Catholic social thought and concrete treatment of various particular moral problems facing the world today. Fundamental to the document is the pope's conviction that authentic human development concerns the whole of the person in every single dimension.

> Without the perspective of eternal life, human progress in this world is denied breathing-space. Enclosed within history, it runs the risk of being reduced to the mere accumulation of wealth; humanity thus loses the courage to be at the service of higher goods, at the service of the great and disinterested initiatives called forth by universal charity. (*CV*, 11)

In his integration of a deep life of faith with a commitment to work to improve justice in the world, Pope Benedict reaffirms the Catholic tradition's rejection of two limits on religious faith. Some limit faith to an internal, spiritual experience in a world where so many of the people of the Earth are unable to meet their basic needs. Others limit faith to a this-worldly zeal for humanizing life in a world where so many people fail to order earthly goals to our higher destiny of life with God. As the pope has put it,

> Man's earthly activity, when inspired and sustained by charity, contributes to the building of the universal city of God, which is the goal of the history of the human family. In an increasingly globalized society, the common good and the effort to obtain it

> cannot fail to assume the dimensions of the whole human family, that is to say, the community of peoples and nations, in such a way as to shape the earthly city in unity and peace, rendering it to some degree an anticipation and a prefiguration of the undivided city of God. (*CV*, 7)

It is out of this integrated view of what authentic development means—for both nations and individuals—that this volume of essays has arisen.

THE INSTITUTE FOR ADVANCED CATHOLIC STUDIES

The Institute for Advanced Catholic Studies was founded to cultivate deep conversation among scholars of diverse backgrounds by bringing the rich Catholic intellectual tradition into dialogue with the various academic disciplines and with contemporary issues—for the benefit of the Church, other religious believers, and the world at large. This commitment to the common good has generated the Institute's True Wealth of Nations research project, itself dedicated to a dialogue on the principles of Catholic social thought and the conditions necessary for a vibrant, creative, and just economy. As Pope Benedict has said, "People in our time feel the need for a new class of intellectuals who can interpret social and cultural dynamics by offering solutions that are practical and realistic, rather than abstract."[1] To engender that dialogue, the project has proposed employing causality as a link between transcendent values and earthly affairs by starting with a bold and as yet untested empirical proposition: "that the economic and cultural criteria identified in the tradition of Catholic social thought provide an effective path to sustainable prosperity for all."

The first undertaking of the True Wealth project was a conference addressing the project's basic assumptions and challenges. Occurring in June 2008 at the University of Southern California, the conference helped to set the agenda for the longer-term project and eventuated in the volume *The True Wealth of Nations: Catholic Social Thought and Economic Life* (Oxford University Press, 2010).

The appearance of *Caritas in veritate* in the summer of 2009 led to the second phase of the project—and a symposium on the relevance of the encyclical for the United States, cosponsored by the Institute for Advanced Catholic Studies and the Pontifical Council for Justice and Peace.

In the apostolic constitution *Pastor Bonus,* Pope John Paul II described the mandate of the Pontifical Council for Justice and Peace to include the work of scholars: "It will assemble and evaluate various types of information and the results of research on justice and peace, the development of peoples and the violations of human rights."[2] For this reason, the council periodically convenes groups of scholars to reflect on pressing issues in the light of both Catholic social thought and the insights of the various scholarly disciplines. Thus, to cosponsor a symposium on *Caritas in veritate* was a natural part of that mission.

THE SYMPOSIUM

The symposium "*Caritas in veritate* and the United States" itself took place at the offices of the Pontifical Council in Rome, October 15–16, 2010. In preparation, the two dozen participants from three continents each wrote a ten-page paper addressing the encyclical and themes within it that called for extension or critique. The papers were circulated and read by all beforehand, so that no time would be needed during the symposium for the presentation of papers or lectures. The time was used instead in a thoughtful and lively interdisciplinary conversation about those critical themes.

This volume begins with a review of the situation in which *Caritas in veritate* appeared, including some of the particular conditions of the United States that affect the ability to hear and act upon the teaching that Pope Benedict proposes (chapter 1). Succeeding chapters address the encyclical's theological grounding (chapter 2) and its view of the relation of economic markets and government (chapter 3). The single most fundamental contribution of the encyclical to the ongoing discussion about morality and economic life arises from its attempt to reconceive "relation" (chapter 4). This entails a rethinking of relationships in economic life and a stress on the importance of reciprocity there (chapter 5), understanding this form of relationship as a mixture of market exchange (where equivalents are exchanged with precision) and a pure gift (where something is transferred with no expectation of any transfer in the other direction).

Caritas in veritate has very important implications for business (chapter 6) and economic development (chapter 7) and for our hope to reduce the polarization of public discourse in the United States, both within the nation and the Church in America (chapter 8). Critical to the encyclical's infrastructure is the language employed, including its ambiguities (chapter 9). The encyclical has implications for a wide range of issues, from personal life to legal systems, welfare policies, and the influence of Catholic social thought in higher education (chapter 10). The book concludes with a review of the place of *Caritas in veritate* in the tradition of Catholic social thought (chapter 11).

A NOTE ABOUT THE TEXT

This is an unusual book, in the sense that each of the chapters includes the work of several authors, with the work of many authors appearing in more than one chapter. There are two primary reasons for this method of presentation of the insights of the symposium. The first is that volumes of conference papers are often less interesting than a volume by a single author on the same topics. Conference volumes sometimes lack thematic integrity. The process employed here provides the book with an intellectual coherence often not available to a collection of conference papers.

The second great benefit of this process is that, page for page, there are simply more good and interesting ideas than appear in most books written by a single author. The reason is that each author was writing a personal reaction to the encyclical, bringing to bear the best of personal strengths and experience. Whether the theme of a chapter is the relation of markets and government, the role of reciprocity in the economy, or the polarization in Church and society, those addressing the theme were the ones with the most interesting things to say about it.

At the same time, however, this approach to the construction of a book generates limitations. The original intention of the symposium was to explore new ground in a situation where no easy synthesis was available. Thus different authors presented sometimes quite different angles on the same general themes. The thematic chapters of this volume require the reader to keep an open mind about the alternative possible approaches to the topic at hand. Whereas a book written by a single author will often take a more singular and focused approach to a theme, this book proposes quite a diversity of disciplinary approaches, certainly a strength in addressing alternative meanings but somewhat less focused than an ordinary book.

Similarly, the reader will need to be prepared for the different styles of writing that characterize the various disciplines from which the authors come. On average, theologians, economists, policy analysts, and philosophers often not only make different sorts of observations about a theme but employ different styles of writing characteristic of their own discipline. In sum, this volume asks the reader to keep an open mind regarding diversity of topics and styles and thereby enter into the richness of perspective that such a process promises.

PARTICIPANTS AND OBSERVERS

Symposium participants included John Allen; Mary Jo Bane; Albino Barrera, OP; Rebecca Blank; Luk Bouchaert; Paul Caron; John A. Coleman, SJ; Paul Dembinski; Miguel Diaz; Daniel Finn; Ruth Groenhout; James Heft, SM; Bryan Hehir; Kenneth Himes, OFM; Mary L. Hirschfeld; David Hollenbach, SJ; Clifford Longley; Katherine Marshall; Bishop William Murphy; Michael Naughton; Michael Novak; Matthew Slaughter; Bishop Mario Toso; Cardinal Peter Turkson; Amy Uelmen; Johan Verstraeten; Alan Wolfe; and Stefano Zamagni; though at the last minute Michael Novak and Alan Wolfe were unable to attend.

Among the observers at the symposium were Francoise Caron, Lewis Ranieri, Thomas and Julie Condon, and Peter and Merle Mullin.

Two staff members from the Pontifical Council, Dr. Flaminia Giovanelli, undersecretary of the council, and Fr. Anthony Frontiero, were a steady and helpful presence.

A DIRECTION FOR THE FUTURE

The final session of the symposium was dedicated to thinking through the themes and issues that need further scholarly analysis and judgment from the Institute, the Pontifical Council, or both. Participants identified a wide range of issues that could benefit from further scholarly attention. Suggestions ranged from gaining a better understanding of economic development of poor nations—and the role of law and a system of jurisprudence in that development—to the spiritual needs of citizens in wealthy nations and the kind of educational efforts that would be required to bring the insights of Catholic social thought into broader use. The most important single theme was to further investigate the moral significance of causality in social and economic life. How should a moral analysis, like that provided in Benedict's encyclical, interact with the empirical analysis provided by the social sciences and policy analysis?

The steering committee of the True Wealth of Nations project is currently developing further the proposals on the relation of ethics and scientific causality. In particular, a project is planned to investigate our moral responsibility for the causal impact of social and economic structures—particularly the harms caused by markets in the lives of the disadvantaged. Other alternatives being investigated are a more general empirical test of the True Wealth assertion that a nation which chooses to follow the proposals of Catholic social thought would be put on a path to sustainable prosperity for all. Such testing could range from the econometric to the experiential and would call on the resources of a number of different scholars in various fields. A third alternative is a deeper study of the role of law in economic development, and in particular the disadvantages that an incomplete system of law imposes upon the poor.

ACKNOWLEDGMENTS

I am vividly aware of debts to many people who made both the symposium and this volume possible. First among these are Cardinal Peter Turkson and Bishop Mario Toso, president and secretary of the Pontifical

Council for Justice and Peace. Their participation in and cosponsorship of the symposium deepened its process and widened its circle of concern. Two others from the council, Dr. Flaminia Giovanelli, undersecretary of the council, and Fr. Anthony Frontiero, provided steady leadership in preparations for the symposium and effective resolution of the logistical problems that such events inevitably entail. I am fundamentally indebted to Paul Caron, codirector with me of the True Wealth of Nations research project, and to Fr. James Heft, SM, president of the Institute for Advanced Catholic Studies. Their wisdom and active leadership made the symposium a forum for vibrant conversation. The success of the symposium depended on the care and attention of many people related to the institute. Thom Rhue, Todd Thaxton, and Gary Adler each played critical roles. Sheila Garrison provided invaluable service in overseeing many arrangements. We are all indebted to several donors to the institute, whose financial support made the symposium possible, including John Kusmiersky, William McKenna Sr., Ellen Hancock, and the Angell Foundation. James Foley has been a great help in proofreading the text, which would not exist at all except for the expert secretarial services of Judy Shank, who not only oversaw the preparation of the manuscript but kept track of a myriad of details. The book itself would not exist without the expert work of many at Oxford University Press, especially Cynthia Read, Charlotte Steinhardt, Karen Fisher, Maureen Cirnitski, Ashwin Bohra and Vivek Lingeswaran. Many hands have contributed to this volume, and I am deeply grateful.

CONCLUSION

Our world today is one of great contrasts, including immense wealth and desperate poverty. Markets are wonderful institutions that elicit hard work and vibrant creativity, which have improved the daily economic well-being of nearly all of humanity. But without a proper juridical framework, strong individual morality, organized care for the poor and unemployed, and a vibrant civil society, markets can also do great harm. In the United States, some who were agents in the creation of the Great Recession of 2008 enjoy immense riches, while a multitude of innocent others have suffered the loss of savings, home, and even self-respect.

The United States remains a place to which a great many people in other nations would love to migrate, but many U.S. citizens feel less economically secure than at any other time in their lives. State governments reduce already meager expenditures on the poorest, while local governments close public libraries on Sunday and reduce the school week from five days to four to save money. In addition, of course, the problems faced by so many millions in poorer areas of the globe are so much more severe as to be daunting even for people of faith.

Any adequate response will require careful attention to both the moral foundations of the economy and the empirical insight provided by the best of social and physical science. The example provided by Pope Benedict in *Caritas in veritate* holds out hope to all of us, hope rooted in the creative love of God and the redemptive life of Jesus Christ. Discerning the meaning of that love and life for our world today remains at the center of the focus of both the Institute for Advanced Catholic Studies and the Pontifical Council for Justice and Peace.

Daniel Finn
Collegeville, Minnesota
January 2011

Chapter 1

The Situation

> The complexity and gravity of the present economic situation rightly cause us concern, but we must adopt a realistic attitude as we take up with confidence and hope the new responsibilities to which we are called by the prospect of a world in need of profound cultural renewal, a world that needs to rediscover fundamental values on which to build a better future.
>
> —Benedict XVI, *Caritas in veritate*, 21

From the time when Pope Leo XIII responded to the abuses of the Industrial Revolution with his 1891 encyclical *Rerum novarum*, modern Catholic social teaching has always taken seriously the promise and problems facing ordinary people. In turn, our own assessment of the situation must consider our social, political, and economic circumstances as well as the ecclesial context of the work of Pope Benedict XVI.

This means that as we begin this engagement with Catholic social thought in *Caritas in veritate*, it will be helpful to attend to the place of Benedict's encyclical within the trajectory of prior social encyclicals, along with a thoughtful look at our own situation, from the American character and the relation of the American people to their government to the basic contours of our economic situation today, both national and global.

The current situation in which we find ourselves is a complex one and thus it will be helpful to consider it from a number of points of view, some quite different from each other. Thus this chapter provides reference to our situation from theological, cultural, and economic perspectives. The diversity presented provides a more robust view of our current context and will make for a firmer foundation for the thematic chapters to come.

CARITAS IN VERITATE IN BROADER CONTEXT

J. BRYAN HEHIR

In the year following the appearance of *Caritas in veritate, Theological Studies*, the premier journal of Catholic theology in the United States, published seven major articles on the encyclical, giving us a sense of the range of commentary that followed the letter. One central topic addressed was whether *Caritas in veritate* stood principally in a line of continuity or discontinuity with previous papal social teaching.

Bernard Laurent argued that the encyclical subscribed "to the logic of the previous social encyclicals," but within that linkage it also "turns the Church's focus away from the interplay of structural forces and gives primacy, as never before, to individual responsibility."[1] Drew Christiansen, SJ, reads the encyclical with different emphasis on both points. He concludes his commentary by citing "the significance for the Church's social ministry of the continuity in the tradition that Benedict has firmly established between Paul VI, John Paul II (in *Laborem exercens* and *Sollicitudo rei socialis*) and his own teaching."[2] He also found in *Caritas in veritate* substantial emphasis on institutional analysis, asserting that "the pope clearly affirms the Church's social mission as dealing with structural change." Christiansen also cites the pope's warning against trying to divide Catholic social teaching into pre- and postconciliar phases of development.

There is much evidence to support Benedict XVI's standing in substantial continuity with the encyclical tradition, a position John Paul II often stressed in his teaching. At the same time, it is both justifiable and necessary to trace the development of papal teaching in light of the problems and challenges facing Catholic social teaching throughout the last century and in the first decade of this one. By itself, such a division will not resolve the differences between Laurent and Christiansen, but it provides a different lens through which the development of papal teaching can be analyzed.

There were three phases of twentieth-century Catholic social teaching, responding to three distinctive challenges in politics, economics, and international relations. The first challenge, the Industrial

Revolution, was the focus of the social encyclicals of Leo XIII, Pius XI, and the Pentecost address of Pius XII. The categories developed in this period (just wage, subsidiarity, social justice) shaped the later social tradition. The focus of the teaching was socioeconomic in content, and the unit of analysis was primarily nations undergoing deep economic changes.

The second challenge, beginning with Pius XII and continuing through John Paul II, was the internationalization of politics, economics, and war, beginning with World War II and continuing through the Cold War. The teaching covered all three topics in a new setting. The theme of much papal teaching was that the emergence of a truly global international system required a moral vision and a political-legal order that could address changing patterns of sovereignty, the emergence of international institutions, and new security threats in the nuclear age.

The third stage in the social teaching was less visible and less distinct than the first two. It involved an address by the Church to the realities of "postindustrial society." The phrase is a product of social science; it focuses upon those nations which first passed through the Industrial Revolution but which by the 1970s possessed very different characteristics. Broadly speaking, these were the wealthy nations of the world, societies with complex social structures, advanced technology, and some version of both a complex market economy and a welfare state. In Catholic social teaching, beginning with *Octogesima adveniens* and continuing through *Centesimus annus*, one can find the Church explicitly engaging the problems, the possibilities, and the responsibilities within these nations and the wider global society.

John Paul II's *Centesimus annus* fulfills the dual role of closing the third stage of the social teaching and opening its fourth stage of development. Written after the end of the Cold War, addressing the emerging fact of globalization, and recognizing the conditions of continuing dehumanizing poverty and societies of great abundance, *Centesimus annus* can be read as the first of the social encyclicals moving toward a new century and a different world order.

The social teaching of Benedict XVI fits squarely within this fourth stage of development. Claims of continuity and discontinuity can both be advanced with reason. Not surprisingly, there is much in the encyclical which draws from prior papal teaching. But Benedict also brings to his teaching role the highly developed skills of a systematic theologian and his own deep convictions about the needs of the Church and the world.

Caritas in veritate has appropriately been classified as the first social encyclical of Benedict XVI. While true in a strict sense, such a designation may fail to acknowledge the social dimensions of Pope Benedict's previous encyclicals. Popes bring their professional background and past experiences to bear upon their social teaching. Pius XII, John XXIII, and Paul VI were experienced diplomats. John Paul II brought the perspective of a moral philosopher and an embattled pastor in a communist state to the Chair of Peter. Benedict's extensive record of theological work provides a distinctive background for approaching an arena (social teaching) that has not been a central theme in his writing. It is all the more significant, therefore, that he chose to emphasize the social character of Catholic faith in each of his three encyclicals.

While he addresses many specific social issues in *Caritas in veritate,* his broader thematic vision may in the long run be his most important contribution to the social tradition. First, in *Deus caritas est,* he synthesized with new emphasis an argument that has been alive in the Church since the *Gaudium et spes* of Vatican II: how to integrate the Church's social ministry and its multiple works of justice and peace with other central dimensions of Catholic faith. With precision and emphasis, he joins social ministry with the sacramental and scriptural dimensions of the Church's life. His encyclicals provide ecclesiological grounding for social teaching and social ministry. Second, he returns regularly to the issue of theological anthropology as the foundation of the Church's understanding of sociopolitical life at every level. This idea, stressed also by *Gaudium et spes* and John Paul II, offers a balanced framework in addressing both the possibilities and the abiding limits of social reform and change. A Christian theological anthropology is always infused by hope, providing a realistic but not a pessimistic sense of effecting change in domestic and world politics. Third, Benedict advances his social teaching with a subtle approach to two realities. On one hand is the dynamic relationship between domestic factors and international relations; he is very conscious of how national boundaries are real and influential but also now porous and less definitive in their influence.

On the other hand, he shows an acute sense of the need to join the Church's social teaching with its ministry of interfaith collaboration. In a post-9/11 world, this initiative is fundamental.

Encyclicals are not written for one part of the Church or the world. Addressed to the whole Church, and more recently to the world as a dialogue partner, the arguments of an encyclical must, by nature, move at a high level of generality. But they are also meant to speak to local churches throughout the world and to illuminate, in religious and moral terms, specific issues of war and peace, wealth and poverty, law and culture. Hence, they require interpretation and application to specific nations, regions, and continents. These tasks of analysis and commentary engage the talents of laity and clergy, of religious and secular voices, of theology, ethics, and various social sciences.

WHO ARE THE AMERICANS?

AMELIA J. UELMEN

> The American is a new man, who acts upon new principles; he must therefore entertain new ideas, and form new opinions. From involuntary idleness, servile dependence, penury, and useless labour, he has passed to toils of a very different nature, rewarded by ample subsistence.—This is an American.[3]

With these words, the French immigrant J. Hector St. Jean de Crèvecoeur in 1782 caught the pulse of what would remain a strong cultural vein: the tendency to throw off old ways of being to embrace the new, pushing beyond settled boundaries and patterns in the quest to claim those "certain unalienable rights" of "life, liberty and the pursuit of happiness."[4] As Crèvecoeur observed, the United States was also a place in which many experienced a new relationship with labor and material goods. "We are all animated with the spirit of an industry which is unfettered and unrestrained, because each person works for himself."[5]

These cultural features—the tendency to push off the old in order to define for oneself the new, and a spirit of "unfettered and unrestrained" industry as we work for ourselves—have been a source of immense positive energy, optimism, and creativity as well as a harmful push toward individual isolation. As another Frenchman, Alexis de Tocqueville, observed during his U.S. travels in the 1830s: "They are in the habit of always considering themselves in isolation and they willingly fancy that their whole destiny is in their hands. . . . Democracy constantly leads back toward himself alone, and threatens in the solitude of his own heart."[6]

A century and a half later, Robert Bellah and a team of scholars diagnosed the cultural consequences of what they termed "ontological individualism"—"the idea that the individual is the only firm reality."[7] Within this framework, many ordinary Americans had come to see freedom as "self-definition": "you have defined who you are, decided for yourself what you want out of life, free as much as possible from the demands of conformity to family, friends or community."[8]

The cultural weave is of course much more complex. One could cite a host of resources and examples that depict how Americans build and value community, often on the foundation of religious vision and conviction.[9] But for purposes of this brief discussion, it is safe to say that the consequences of ontological individualism can make it challenging for many Americans to fully access the framework of *Caritas in veritate*.

These broadly held cultural assumptions can render invisible the transcendent dimension that Benedict's encyclical proposes as grounding for its ethical framework, and can prevent any reimagining of our connections to others and to the common good. In short, it is extremely difficult for so many of our fellow citizens to find an effective entry point into the riches of Benedict's document.

AMERICANS AND GOVERNMENT TODAY

REBECCA M. BLANK

The first decade of the twenty-first century has been unsettling in many ways. The economic and social reality that surrounds many Americans has changed substantially in a very short period of time. The emergence of international terrorist organizations has increased Americans' sense of personal vulnerability and has led to a noticeable increase in governmentally designated surveillance of and restrictions on citizen behavior. The recent collapse of financial markets and the subsequent deep recession have increased Americans' sense of economic insecurity. The rising debate over global environmental change and the threat of global climate disruptions have increased Americans' sense of uncertainty about the future facing their children. One claim of government is that it exists to make citizens' lives safer and better, yet in this past decade, government responses have often seemed inadequate in the face of such immense problems.

Dramatic changes in information and communication technologies have also occurred at almost dizzying speed, creating a gulf between the daily habits of those who are "connected" and those who are not. The technological changes of the last two decades have occurred hand in hand with major changes in the global interconnectedness of businesses and national economies.

It is perhaps not surprising that a rising sense of change, insecurity, and threat have made Americans more hostile to and more demanding of those who promise to make it right. And the rising tide of distrust of government is not new in the last decade, but part of a longer-term decline in trust in public institutions that has been ongoing for several decades. Yet this creates serious challenges for effective governance. Anger at elected officials, an antitax movement, and general hostility towards those viewed as government insiders can make it difficult for even some of the usual activities of government to occur, much less for political institutions to move forward in addressing new and complex challenges. Ironically, declining trust in government makes it harder for public institutions to operate effectively, just at the moment when the need for effective government action may be rising.

Government in a democracy does not exist in a realm separate from citizen beliefs and actions. With rising distrust of public institutions, the only effective response by public leaders must be transparency and leadership. Transparency in the functioning and behavior of public institutions is as important as transparency in the actions of their leadership. Political leaders must speak truth, so far as they understand it, if they are to regain citizen confidence. Confidence in government can erode quickly but can only be rebuilt slowly, over time. Pope Benedict's encyclical *Caritas in veritate* discusses the religious appreciation for community-based organizations and communal solutions. One critical challenge in our day is whether such organizations can act as intermediaries that give citizens a stronger voice in democratic government and thereby facilitate renewed trust.

OUR CURRENT ECONOMIC SITUATION

MATTHEW J. SLAUGHTER

The American economy faces several deep challenges in the wake of the world financial crisis and the Great Recession. These confront any one of us hoping for guidance from Pope Benedict's *Caritas in veritate* or from any other source of religious or secular wisdom.

Federal Reserve Chairman Ben Bernanke has acknowledged that the economic outlook remains unusually uncertain at best. Despite the fact that the National Bureau of Economic Research declared that the Great Recession came to an end in June 2009, economic growth in the United States slowed markedly in 2010. The annualized rate of growth in U.S. gross domestic product fell from 5.0 percent in the fourth quarter of 2009 to 3.7 percent and then just 1.7 percent and 2.5 percent in the first through third quarters of 2010.[10]

For American workers and their families, perhaps the most important challenge is that U.S. companies of all sizes have yet to resume vigorous job creation. From peak to trough, in the Great Recession the U.S. economy lost 8.47 million private-sector payroll jobs—a remarkable 7.3 percent. Currently, the U.S. economy has about 108 million private-sector payroll jobs and 11.7 million manufacturing payroll jobs. When was the last time it had that few? April 1999 and April 1941, respectively. So far in 2010, the entire U.S. nonfarm business sector created an average of only 111,500 payroll jobs per month.[11] This is far fewer than are needed just to accommodate population growth, let alone to refill the jobs hole the United States now finds itself in—a hole that will likely take many, many years to fill.

But the labor market challenges facing the United States are not confined to just the number of jobs. A deep challenge also exists regarding the kind of jobs available: the real and relative earnings performance of most Americans has been poor for many years.

The data are sobering. Recently released IRS data show that in 2008 the share of gross personal income accounted for by the top 1 percent of tax filers (i.e., by those reporting at least $368,238 in income that year) stood at 21.0 percent, down slightly from 23.5 percent the previous year. These levels come after thirty years of ongoing increases in income concentration—in 1977 the top 1 percent got just 7.9 percent of all personal income—and today are close to the record levels of income inequality of the late 1920s.

And in many ways even more troubling, U.S. inequality is widening largely because of falling real incomes for all but the most-skilled highest earners. Consider the information shown in table 1.1 on the change from 2000 through 2009 in median real (i.e., inflation adjusted) total money earnings for working adults (aged twenty-five years and above) by educational cohort (the best single measure of worker skills).

Table 1.1 MEDIAN REAL TOTAL MONEY EARNINGS FOR WORKING ADULTS (AGE TWENTY-FIVE AND ABOVE) BY EDUCATIONAL COHORT, 2000–2009

Educational Group	*U.S. Employment Share (%)*	*Earnings Change 2000–2009 (%)*
No high school degree	8.7	–10.0
High school diploma	28.8	–9.4
Some college	27.5	–6.6
Four-year college degree	22.5	–5.5
Master's degree	8.9	–1.3
Doctoral degree	1.8	+1.8
Doctors, lawyers, and MBAs	1.8	+11.1

From 2000 through 2009, only workers with a doctorate or a professional postgraduate degree—just 3.6 percent of the labor force—enjoyed increases in their average real money incomes. All other educational cohorts, including college graduates and those with nonprofessional master's degrees, suffered declines here. The Great Recession may put further downward pressure on the earnings of most Americans for many years.

This sobering picture for the earnings of individual workers translates into a similarly dismal view of the earnings for families. In 2009, the median American household earned $49,777 in income. This fell by a sharp 4.2 percent in the next two years alone. Following sluggish performance in earlier years, today's median household income is barely above where it was in 1997.

This overall picture of the pressures on U.S. workers and their families is shocking. Today there are fewer private-sector jobs than there were a decade ago, and the real earnings of nearly all these jobs today are less than they were a decade ago. Over the twentieth century, only the Great Depression produced worse economic results. Millions of American families face real hardship. For my own two sons and all other children in America, I am deeply concerned. The human and political-economy ramifications of falling incomes continue to be what grays my hair more than any other policy issue in America.

Beyond the immediate pressures on workers, their families, and communities, these income trends are linked to a protectionist drift in U.S. economic policy seen, for example, in the 2009 Employ American Workers Act. Public support for beneficial international trade and globalization is strongly linked to labor market performance, which has been weak for so long. A strong protectionist drift will harm all.

So, what to do? Policymakers have long quibbled over the facts. They have also invoked vague and distant remedies. Better educate the U.S. workforce? Upgrading skills is terrific, especially for teachers like me. But this takes generations. It took over sixty years for the United States to boost its college graduate labor force share from about 6 percent in 1945 to the approximately 33 percent it is today—and that entailed major government programs (such as the GI Bill) and profound socioeconomic changes (such as rising female education and labor force participation). Education alone would simply be too little, too late.

More fundamentally, the question of what to do is difficult to answer because academic research has yet to definitively evaluate the relative contribution of forces such as innovation in companies' products and processes spurred by information technology capital, rising health care costs, immigration inflows, and international trade and investments—especially as related to fast-growing developing nations such as China and India. Almost surely globalization has played some role in these income trends. It is hard not to juxtapose the data in table 1.1 with the post-2000 surge of China into the global economy, spurred by its 2001 accession to the World Trade Organization and by its stunningly fast rate of overall economic growth during that period, in excess of 10 percent per year.

But at some point, American workers and families will demand an answer—both directly and indirectly through the voice of their elected officials. How will policymakers respond? How should they respond? What guidance might *Caritas in veritate* provide us for understanding responsibility for and responses to the labor market pressures that face Americans in the wake of the Great Recession?

Particularly relevant here is the following passage. "The sharing of goods and resources, from which authentic development proceeds, is not guaranteed by merely technical progress and relationships of utility, but by the potential of love that overcomes evil with good (cf. *Rom* 12:21), opening up the path towards reciprocity of consciences and liberties" (*CV*, 9). What if the market outcomes of earnings presented in table 1.1 were to persist in the United States for another year? Another decade? Longer? What role for "love" would the United States be able to summon to address such hardship?

Pope Benedict rightly deplores "the scandal of glaring inequalities" (*CV*, 22), and he later cautions that inequalities can grow too large and thereby damage social capital and even democracy itself: "The dignity of the individual and the demands of justice require, particularly today, that economic choices do not cause disparities in wealth to increase in an excessive and morally unacceptable manner" (*CV*, 32). Are U.S. earnings now "excessively" disparate? And he further states in no uncertain terms: "I would like to remind everyone, especially governments engaged in boosting the world's economic and social assets, that the *primary capital to be safeguarded and valued is man, the human person in his or her integrity*: Man is the source, the focus and the aim of all economic and social life" (*CV*, 25, emphasis in the original). Discerning the obligations of individuals, businesses, and government in our hard economic times is wisely part of the pope's agenda and a challenge for us all.

GLOBAL ECONOMIC FORCES

ALBINO BARRERA

Contemporary globalization actually entails two separate but complementary phenomena: global economic integration and the emergence of the knowledge economy. In the same way that cheap cotton cloth, cheap iron and steel, cheap steam power and electricity, and cheap oil gave rise to the modern industrial economy of the last three centuries, so today cheap information is radically altering the way we work, consume, live, and interact with one another.[12] This emerging globalized "knowledge economy" will be as historic and transformative for the postindustrial era as the Industrial Revolution was in shaping modernity centuries ago.

Epochal economic shifts are usually accompanied by changes in the public's market ethos. People's perception of what is right or wrong and what is fair or unfair adjusts in the wake of the damaging effects of paradigm shifts. For example, in response to the abuses during the early phases of the Industrial Revolution, nineteenth-century British social legislation imposed a minimum age for employment, maximum hours and days of work, and workplace safety regulations. These norms eventually became standard for most countries in the twentieth century. Today, we are in the midst of a similar adjustment in market morality.

The market is playing an increasingly central role in shaping and implementing public policy. Note, for example, its impact on international relations (e.g., U.S.-China economic symbiosis) and its role in the pursuit of social goals (e.g., trading in carbon emissions). The market can be a wonderful instrument encouraging creativity and constructive technological change—and it has been a big part of the rise of many nations out of the depths of subsistence agriculture. But the market has also seeped into many facets of our common and private lives (e.g., commercial surrogacy). Left on its own with minimal oversight from the community, the marketplace will impose its own ethos. Since it is focused principally on allocative efficiency, the neoclassical market takes little note of the unintended consequences it spawns, such as materialism, consumerism, impersonalism, and individualism. Unsuspecting market participants will find themselves either internalizing these values by default or reluctantly conforming to them for their own economic survival. Market models and rules bring with them a market mentality, that is, a market-generated morality.[13]

Chapter 2

The Theological Grounding of *Caritas in veritate*

> The correct viewpoint, then, is that of the tradition of the apostolic faith, a patrimony both ancient and new, outside of which . . . issues concerning development would be reduced to merely sociological data.
>
> —Benedict XVI, *Caritas in veritate*, 10

Pope Benedict makes clear in *Caritas in veritate* the theological foundations of Catholic social thought. Our own appropriation and extension of the insights of this tradition, then, must attend to those foundations, in appreciation for their traditional wisdom about God and humanity's place in creation and in extension and critique of how this particular encyclical construes the fundamentals out of which lives of faith and action must arise.

Thus an investigation of those theological foundations should start with situating Benedict's theological framework within the recent history of the Church and even within his own history as a theologian whose views have developed over a half century. Basic themes of grace, sin, and the Christian view of the person are central. And important questions about the adequacy of the encyclical can be pressed about the relation of charity and justice and the role of the poor in the proper development of Catholic theology. The authors in this chapter address a wide range of topics very helpful for understanding the theological background of Pope Benedict's encyclical. The diversity of perspectives and the presence of an appreciative critique of Benedict's arguments will be most helpful in situating the treatment of themes later in this volume.

SITUATING POPE BENEDICT'S THEOLOGY

BISHOP WILLIAM F. MURPHY

The clear and unambiguous introduction of properly theological categories into Pope Benedict's "social encyclical," *Caritas in veritate,* is striking. Every social encyclical since Pope Leo XIII's *Rerum novarum* has included a brief but important section on the relation between justice and charity. Thus it would be inappropriate to dismiss earlier encyclicals as lacking a properly theological matrix. Yet the introduction of theological categories by Benedict is bold and innovative.

In *Solicitudo rei socialis,* Pope John Paul II included a chapter called "A Theological Reading of Modern Problems." Therein he gave a stimulating proposal for the move from interdependence to solidarity as a process that had within itself the potential to open up to the deeper theological characteristic of *communio,* the communion that unites us with the Triune God and can become the foundation for validating and furthering human solidarity as a virtue.

Benedict, however, is mining new ground, confident that the incarnate Son of God reveals that everything human has a relation to the divine, including markets, financial institutions, and globalized economic relationships. The pope speaks of the principle of gratuitousness, the logic of gift, solidarity, and communion, and charity in truth. He introduces God as a dynamic element in the political, economic, and social order, and not simply as the reference point for individual virtue and personal faith.

The promise of this document resides in its concern for true freedom and for the necessity of God in our individual and communal lives, without whom human beings ultimately become enslaved to ideologies and institutions that demean the dignity and transcendent character of human life. This theological grounding of *Caritas in veritate* provides real hope in confronting the immense problems we face today.

DEVELOPMENTS IN POPE BENEDICT'S THINKING

JOHN A. COLEMAN

By almost any reckoning of the tradition of papal social encyclicals, *Caritas in veritate* provides the best-developed theological argument for the grounding of Catholic social teaching. The introduction (*CV*, 1–9) spells out a theological anthropology based on the *logos-agape* quality of God the creator, whom Benedict has elsewhere referred to as "a Freedom who Thinks."[1] This theology also draws on a rich sense of grace as gift, such that life itself can be seen as a gift—a superabundance received and passed on with a gratuitousness that exceeds any mere logic of recompense (*CV*, 34, 52). The human "search for love and truth is purified and liberated by Jesus Christ from the impoverishment that our humanity brings to it, and he reveals to us in all its fullness the initiative of love and the plan for true life that God has prepared for us" (*CV*, 1).

Prior to Vatican Council II, Catholic social teaching rested strongly on a notion of natural law and the requirement that societies be structured in accord with justice and the common good. *Caritas in veritate* instead lifts up a developed notion of charity (divine love communicated to humans as grace) as at the heart of the Church's social doctrine (*CV*, 2). It postulates that the human can attain the natural and supernatural truth of charity: grasping its meaning as gift, acceptance, and communion (*CV*, 3). Love and truth are closely intertwined. Charity is love received and given; it is grace (*CV*, 4). A theology of grace as God's superabundant love communicated to humans suffuses the encyclical. Grace is firmly planted in the introduction to the encyclical, is reprised in a middle section (*CV*, 38), and is once again appealed to in the conclusion (*CV*, 78).

The encyclical, then, expounds how "truth frees charity from the constraints of emotionalism that deprives it of relational and social content and of a fideism that deprives it of human and universal breathing-space" (*CV*, 3). Here is a classic treatment of how love and justice correlate. Love presumes but surpasses, corrects, and goes beyond mere human justice (*CV*, 6). Indeed, in one sentence that sounds to some a bit like Christian triumphalism, it is claimed that "adhering to the values of Christianity is not merely useful but essential for building a good society and for true integral human development" (*CV*, 4). As the pope explains, "because it is a gift received by everyone, charity in truth is a force that builds community; it brings all people together without imposing barriers or limits. . . . Economic, social and political development, if it is to be authentically human, needs to make room for the principle of gratuitousness as an expression of fraternity" (*CV*, 34).

So where does this emphasis on a theological base for Catholic social thought come from? Already toward the end of the Second Vatican Council, Joseph Ratzinger had bluntly remarked: "A proper theological social doctrine does not exist, though the attempt at the ever new 'evangelization' in man's concrete social history does exist."[2] More recently, Ratzinger showed a readiness to move beyond appeal to the natural law, because "its blades have become blunt at a time when, with the victory of the theory of evolution, the idea of nature's rationality has become obsolete."[3]

Nonetheless, Benedict maintains one of the primary claims of the natural law tradition:

> In all cultures there are examples of ethical convergence, some isolated, some interrelated, as an expression of the one human nature willed by the Creator; the tradition of ethical wisdom knows this as the natural law. This universal moral law provides a sound basis for all cultural, religious, and political dialogue, and it ensures that the multi-faceted pluralism of cultural diversity does not detach itself from the common quest for truth, goodness, and God. Thus, adherence to the law etched on human hearts is the precondition for all constructive social cooperation. (*CV*, 59)

To be sure, classic Catholic construals of natural law always included a theological appeal. "Human dignity"—a key component of the social teaching—implicitly assumed the notion of the *imago Dei* as well as Catholic communitarian motifs of a solidarity that respects personhood, mirroring more fundamental concepts of *communio* in the inner life of the Trinity.[4] So it is a conspicuous achievement of *Caritas in veritate* to have provided us with a more full-fledged and fully theological grounding of Catholic social thought. This remains true even though Benedict has selected only some of a number of possible theological themes for this grounding. As Lisa Cahill has argued, Benedict's word-agape Christology does not exhaust the full theological meaning of Christ and may miss elements that would be more readily found in other Christological titles: Son of Man and Eschatological Judge, High Priest, Lord, Envoy of Divine Wisdom, Messiah, and The Crucified, Risen, and Exalted One.[5] Citing Thomas Reese, Cahill suggests such alternative Christologies might yield some greater expectations for this-worldly social change.[6]

Another limitation entailed in Benedict's development of a more explicitly theological foundation for Catholic social teaching is that some of the notions grounded in theology are not unique to Catholic theology or could at least also be articulated in more secular humanistic language. Thus, for example, Benedict asserts that "the Christian revelation of the unity of the human race presupposes a metaphysical interpretation of the 'humanum' in which relationality is an essential element" (*CV*, 55). But a number of non-Christian accounts of the "humanum" also postulate relationality as an essential element.[7] The insight is essential for Christians but not unique to Christianity. One advantage to the natural law approach is the recognition that many fundamental characteristics of human life—human existence as a gift and humans as givers—can but do not have to be described in explicitly Christian theological terms.

A THEOLOGY OF GRATUITOUSNESS

PAULINUS I. ODOZOR

Pope Benedict's *Caritas in veritate* presents us with a lively and wide-ranging understanding of gift—of the theology, ethics, and economics of gratuitousness. Gary Anderson's recent book, *Sin: A History,* makes an important contribution to this development, pointing to a rich biblical foundation for economic metaphors related to sin, redemption, and Christian action.

Anderson's book focuses us on the debt of our sins, relieved through Christ's atonement, as emphasized by early eastern Christian writers like Ephrem the Syrian,[8] for whom alms and loans to the poor are a testimony to faith and a sacrifice to God.[9] Yet as Anderson explains, "what God offers far exceeds what human beings provide in exchange. In the enacting of any of these modalities of relationship one is taught the radical dependence of the creature upon his creator."[10]

In charity, we enact God's grace toward the poor as repayment for sin, as shown in the story of Nebuchadnezzar,[11] in which the prophet Daniel, in an attempt to help Nebuchadnezzar avert the catastrophe predicted in the king's dream, said to him, "Therefore, O King, take my advice: atone for your sins by good deeds, and for your misdeeds by kindness to the poor. Then your prosperity will be long" (Dan. 4:24).

Many other ancient writers also suggested that alms escaped the zero-sum game of the ancient economy, sharing Pope Benedict's view that ethical economic action like development aid helps all parties. In a Christian vein, one receives a bounteous rate of interest when lending to God.[12] For Clement of Alexandria, one can "buy a heavenly kingdom" through the human act of thanksgiving.[13] For Augustine, as for many of the Fathers, even the relationship between God and humanity is marked by reciprocity and gratuitousness. Augustine urges his listeners to "study the money-lender's methods. He wants to give modestly and get back with profit; you do the same. Give a little and receive on a grand scale. Look how your interest is mounting up! Give temporal wealth and claim eternal increase; give the earth and gain heaven!"[14]

An economics of gratuitousness is essential to development properly understood, and so development requires "a transcendent vision of the person; it needs God." For only "through encounter with God are we able to see in the other more than just another creature . . ." (*CV*, 11) and only through an appreciation of our debt to God can we grasp the ethics and the economics of gratuitousness that *Caritas in veritate* advocates. The problem is how this can be achieved in an economy which, as the pope himself points out, is used to running on its own principles, without God and sometimes without the appreciation of anything but profits and the laws of supply and demand. The truth, according to Pope Benedict, is that such a view of economics is unsustainable without a transcendent view of the human person. For although reason by itself is capable of grasping the equality between human beings, "it cannot establish fraternity." Rather, fraternity "originates in a transcendent vocation from God the Father, who loved us first, teaching us through the Son what fraternal charity is" (*CV*, 19).

In addition to being an appeal for a wider understanding and renewal of worldwide economic activity, the pope's call to an ethic and economics of gratuitousness is also a call for Christian witness within the Church in three ways. In the first place, it is a call for a more intense response to the love of God that is made manifest through the stunning deed of God in Jesus Christ. It calls every Christian to a life of generosity that borders on "prodigality," like that of the Father who gives all for nothing and asks for nothing in return (Luke 15:11–31).

Second, the economics and theology of gratuitousness in this encyclical are a summons to the entire Church to examine its internal life. The gifts of God that have been given to various parts of the Church must also be shared with other parts in gratitude to God the giver. The Church must be acutely sensitive to the disparities within its walls to make sure no one part of the Church—nation, diocese, or parish—has it all while the rest have little or nothing. This pertains to all goods, economic and spiritual. The Petrine office in this regard must continue to see itself as redistributionist in chief. It must continue to insist, for example, that those parts of the Church with abundant personnel share them with others. The same goes for other parts of the Church that have abundant economic or other resources. The Petrine office thus helps the entire Church to share grace, wealth, joy, and sorrow. In this way, the Church is able to model the fullness of charity and truth, expressing in its every prayer and action the perfection and beauty of God's communion with humanity in Christ, and in him with one another.

Third, therefore, an ethics of gratuitousness summons the Church to intensify its efforts in the work of advocacy for those who are voiceless, regardless of their faith, ethnicity, or other affiliations, in response to the God whose love for us is boundless.

If Catholicism in America appears sometimes to be a lone voice among other Christian groups, it is precisely because, like the rest of the Catholic Church, it is grateful for ancient, profound, and transcendent gifts and not simply for recent things. Gratuitousness, as the pope describes it, presupposes a long but too often interrupted memory of

God's gracious action in history. Ancient Israel possessed this memory as a living thing. That is why that nation at its best had gratuitousness enshrined in its laws and commandments. The Church possesses that memory, keeps it alive, and makes it present through its preaching and rituals. Indeed the Church's work of charity presupposes this reality, as Pope Benedict noted in his first encyclical, *Deus caritas est*. Although the Catholic culture of Europe did much to perpetuate this memory of God's action in the world, much of this memory is lost in contemporary Europe through a secularism that is not merely a denial of the existence of God but a true disruption of the people's memory of God's gratuitous action in the world, the very basis of the ethics and economics of gratuity that the pope advocates in his encyclical.

BENEDICT'S VIEW OF THE PERSON

KENNETH R. HIMES

At Vatican II the assembled bishops articulated a consistent theme of Catholic social teaching in *Gaudium et spes*: "The human person is the source, the focus and the aim of all economic and social life" (*GS*, 63). Few would deny the claim, but the crucial area for debate is one's understanding of the human person. This is where Benedict departs from many defenders of the present economic order, for he finds fault with the way that our global market system is evolving, and the fault is ultimately one of anthropology.

In *Centesimus annus*, Pope John Paul II analyzed the collapse of Soviet communism and, while acknowledging the "inefficiency of the economic system," pointed out that failing alone did not explain the collapse. There was also the error of a misguided view of the person, one that denied people a proper and necessary freedom, that viewed the human "on the basis of economics alone," thereby ignoring the cultural and spiritual aspects of the individual (*CA*, 24). Just as John Paul saw the error of anthropology undermining communism, Benedict in *Caritas in veritate* argues that a mistaken view of the human person undercuts our own economic order. Today human development "runs the risk of being reduced to the mere accumulation of wealth" (*CV*, 11). In developing this mode of critique, Benedict echoes Paul VI and John Paul II, contrasting the vision of integral human development in Catholic social thought with a reductionist view of the person. The present economic crisis is due, in part, to the pursuit of profit as an economic goal without regard for the common good or the appropriate means of pursuing economic gain (*CV*, 21). And the overly narrow pursuit of profit, ignoring other, broader goals of human advancement, is fed by an ideology that reduces the human to but one aspect of the human person.

Benedict follows the tradition of Catholic social thought when asserting that *homo economicus* is an incomplete anthropology. To reduce human motivation and thought to that of a rational maximizer of self-interest is to truncate the nature of the human and to misread the aim of authentic human development. Human beings, of course, do demonstrate self-interest in their attitudes and behaviors. Yet humans are complex beings who act for a variety of reasons, and a more adequate market economy will make room for a wider range of human motives to be considered.[15]

As Pope Benedict and his predecessors maintain, the person is capable of transcendence, moving beyond self-interest and pure materialism. For example, Benedict maintains the social nature of the human is a witness to the image of God in which we are created, reflecting the Trinitarian communion of divine persons (*CV*, 54). To ignore the importance of social relationships, the common good, and solidarity for the sake of maximizing profit is to misinterpret the meaning of human development by overlooking the essential relatedness of the person.

The importance of an adequate view of persons and their authentic development leads the pope to several pointed criticisms of common public and corporate policies. Driven by a narrow pursuit of profit, companies engage in never-ending searches for sources of cheap labor and the outsourcing of production to locales where workers' rights are abused, social security systems are downsized, and fundamental aspirations of people are crushed (*CV*, 25).

Shortsighted economic thinking that prizes maximizing profit above all else has also produced long-term unemployment among segments of the population, a particularly painful form of economic marginalization. This phenomenon "undermines the freedom and creativity of the person" along with that of the family and other social relations, "causing great psychological and spiritual suffering." Recalling John Paul II's principle of the priority of labor,[16] Benedict reminds readers "that the primary capital to be safeguarded and valued is the human, the human person in his or her integrity" (*CV,* 25).[17]

Another example of anthropological reductionism in economic life is related to consumerism. The pope notes that "the consumer has a specific social responsibility" to ensure that the proper use of material goods does not deteriorate into a pursuit of ever higher levels of material consumption. Individuals need to be educated about their consumption patterns and acknowledge the moral dimensions of their consumer choices. This becomes difficult, however, when people are encouraged to define themselves by their consumption. The human person is a consumer but that activity ought not be the defining identity of an individual.

It would be easy to multiply examples of Benedict's approach, but it is clear that, according to *Caritas in veritate,* a fundamental issue of anthropology is at stake in today's economic debates. Should profit maximization be an end in itself, or even the highest goal of economic activity? Is human betterment to be equated with "having more" and greater consumption? Or should a broader view of the human person and the common good guide profit making and consumer choice to a different end?

In the face of these distorted images of the human, Benedict warns that "the human consequences of current tendencies towards a short-term economy—sometimes very short-term—need to be carefully evaluated." We need a "further and deeper reflection on the meaning of the economy and its goals, as well as profound and far-sighted revision of the current model of development, so as to correct its dysfunctions and deviations" (*CV,* 32).

CHALLENGES TO BENEDICT'S VISION: SIN

MICHAEL NOVAK

In *Caritas in veritate,* Pope Benedict is bringing the long-neglected lessons of St. Augustine back to Catholic social thought. Benedict re-presents *The City of God,* that is, the City of that *caritas* which the

Divine Persons gratuitously pour into the human heart, that it might cause the burning desire for human unity to kindle hundreds of millions of parched hearts.

Without eternal perspectives and without the sense of our individual immortal value—the great Tocqueville reminded us—the sheer materialism and dreck of democracy and capitalism would wear us down to mean and petty creatures. Materialism radically undercuts our human rights. Simply to survive, let alone flourish, democracy and capitalism need soul.

For Catholics, all social energy flows from the inner life of the Trinity. Everything is gift. We signal our gratitude by developing our own talents to the full, by becoming free, responsible, initiative-showing, creative agents of a better world, and by aspiring to that full communion of all human beings whose vocation is written into the structure of human history.

And we say "thank you." What most distinguishes Jewish and Christian believers from secular materialists is the frequency and the authenticity with which believers respond to everyday events with deeply felt gratitude. Everything we look upon is gift.

Thus, it is no surprise when empirical research shows that people who are believers give more of their time and resources to the needy than do unbelievers, and people who cherish limited government (conservatives) give more of their personal funds to help the poor than do welfare-state liberals. The truth is, though, that both liberals and conservatives belong, in their quarreling fashions, to one same national community, and one same human community.

What Benedict XVI has not spelled out yet is another forgotten lesson from St. Augustine: the ever-corrupting role of sin in the City of Man. Augustine points out how difficult it is even for the wisest and most detached humans to discover the truth among lies—and how even husbands and wives in the closest of human bonds misunderstand each other so often. The Father of Lies seems to own so much of the real world.

What are the most practical ways of defeating sin? The Catholic tradition—even the wise Pope Benedict—still seems to put too much stress upon *caritas*, virtue, justice, and good intentions, and not nearly enough on methods for defeating human sin in all its devious and persistent forms.

For example, the American state differs most from the European state in its very strong expectation of the damage done to societies by original sin. The American founders, like the sixteenth century Reformers generally, were strongly attached to the doctrine of sin in St. Augustine. They understood quite well that every human being sometimes sins. From this they drew a practical conclusion: every human being needs to operate within a system of checks and balances, so that one person's faults or excesses may be checked by the interests and powers of other persons. Both in the economic order and in the political order, Americans carefully constructed these checks and balances in institutional form, so that every institution is checked by at least one other institution (often more). Thus all institutions become sentinels and guardians against the excesses of other institutions.

Given the expectation of universal human sinfulness, there is no use building a system that will work only for saints, for persons who practice all the virtues, for persons infused with *caritas* and justice and all the rest. There are too few such citizens to compose a republic. It is necessary to build republics—and also business systems, scientific systems, and every other kind of system—for sinners. It is the human tendency toward sin that makes the checks and balances of a republic necessary. It is the capacity of human beings for practicing humble virtues most of the time (but not always) that makes republics and other well-protected institutions possible.

There are analogous checks and balances in the business system. Indeed, this is why the American founders preferred a society based on industry and commerce to a society based on an aristocracy or military order. By their very nature, industry competes with industry, and firm with firm. The interests of the highway sector are not the same as those of the builders of canals, which are not the same as the interests of the railroad industry; nor are they the same as those of the airlines. Some of the American states are rich in lumber, others in cotton, others in vegetables and fruits for the table, others in wines or recreational facilities, or iron and steel, or are rich in the accidents of history that allow certain industries to develop within them, such as the manufacturing of automobiles or electronics. Thus the interests of one state lead it to be a rival of and sentinel over the interests of other states. Competition among firms in the same industry makes each of them a rival of and a sentinel over the interests of others.

One does not defeat sin in human beings solely by inculcating the practice of virtues; an even more reliable way of diminishing the effects of sin is by wisely and efficiently creating various systems of checks, balances, competition, and rival interests. In one light, institutional checks are better sentinels against human sin; in another light, the practice of virtues by multitudes of individuals is the better sentinel. Both are necessary.

A foundational problem of economic and political systems based on utopian expectations, or even expectations of prevailing human virtue, is that they are utterly unrealistic about sinful human nature. They are ill founded. They are bound to collapse of their own perfectionism and even willful blindness to flawed human nature. That is why so many political and economic systems in our time have collapsed inward of their own weight.

In short, Catholic social thought needs to pay far more attention than it has to the ravages of original sin in human institutions at every time and in every place. It needs to show more inventiveness and creativity in recognizing and developing the systems of check, balances, and competition that may arise from the resources of human nature itself, even sinful human nature.

THEOLOGICAL FOUNDATIONS OF THE MARKET

ALBINO BARRERA

As Pope Benedict articulates in *Caritas in veritate*, the Catholic social tradition's support of markets is based on both faith and reason. As body and soul, human beings require many material inputs for physical survival and basic health. Human growth and development are even more demanding in their material requirements. To make matters worse, even as legitimate human needs are great, human wants are even greater, perhaps even unlimited. Unfortunately, these simultaneous immense needs and insatiable wants run up against two natural constraints. First, persons working by themselves cannot produce and provide for all their own needs, much less their wants, and second, the goods of the earth are finite.

Human beings get around both constraints through collaborative work. The division of labor is not a uniquely modern phenomenon since it is part of human nature. After all, human beings are social by nature. Of course, the corollary of a division of labor is exchange. People trade with each other in order to procure what they are unable to produce by themselves. Such cooperation also serves as a means of getting around the finitude of the earth's resources. People allocate among themselves the limited goods of the earth. As human communities expand in size and complexity, the marketplace has increasingly replaced extended families and clans as the venue for such collaborative work and allocation. Today, the market is the principal terrain for economic cooperation. Note, for example, the phenomena of outsourcing and international vertical integration in which product components come from all over the world (e.g., for airplanes, cars, electronics, and apparel). Markets have turned the whole world into a truly single integrated workshop.

The modern Catholic social tradition supported market operations early on, even if not as explicitly as it later did in *Centesimus annus*. For example, in affirming the right to private property ownership and in arguing that such property ownership is a means of saving and upward mobility for the working poor, *Rerum novarum* implicitly acknowledged a legitimate role for markets in ennobling human life.

The theological foundations of markets have their starting point in the aforesaid pivotal function of markets in providing for human needs and wants. In particular, consider how markets are instrumental in actualizing some of Christian theology's key anthropological presuppositions on the human community. First, in Aristotelean-Thomistic metaphysics, creatures reflect and communicate some dimension of the goodness and perfections of God. They do so according to their mode of being and operation. In living up to this potential, creatures individually and collectively contribute both to the internal order of the universe and to the whole creation's attainment of its external order in God, its final end.

In the case of human beings, their mode of being and operation lies in their moral agency and reaches its full natural potential in moral excellence. Similarly, in acting as a group, human beings raise their communication of some aspect of the goodness and perfections of God to a new dimension. A morally excellent human community has its own unique contribution to make to the internal order of the universe and to the attainment of creation's final end in God. Economic life, including markets, is a constitutive element of human life and community. In other words, the market (as a collaborative effort of moral agents) has its own requisite share in reflecting some dimension of God's goodness and perfections. Thus, markets function properly only as they operate according to the end for which they were created, that is, to contribute toward the internal and external order of creation. In fact, markets are important because they can provide propitious conditions in facilitating peoples' attainment of moral excellence.

Second, markets contribute to bringing to completion the one Body that we are. Though we are many members, each with unique gifts, we nonetheless form and serve the One Body of Christ (Rom. 12:3–8). Our gifts are put at the service of others and the whole community. Economic exchange is a means by which we actualize this reality. Note, for example, Paul's collection among the Gentile churches for the poor of Jerusalem (e.g., 1 Cor. 16:1–3), his own employment to prevent his being a burden to the churches he served (1 Thess. 2:6–9), and the Pauline insistence that people earn a livelihood for their own keep (2 Thess. 3:11–12).

Third, the human community is not contractual but is familial in nature (*Gaudium et spes*). Specialization, division of labor, interdependence, and exchange become occasions by which economic activity builds relationships and communities. And because we are family, such economic exchange is ultimately rooted in charity rather than in contracts. Thus, Christian social thought has consistently taught that economic life finds its crown in self-giving and in unmeasured generosity, rather than in acquisitive accumulation or in overindulgent consumption.

Fourth, economic agency is an essential means by which we actualize two signal divine benefactions: (1) the gift of material sufficiency for all our needs, and (2) the gift of participating in God's governance and providence. God provides for us through nature and, more significantly, through each other. As human beings, we are not merely instruments of God's providence. We are, in fact, secondary causes because we add something that is uniquely our own and freely given—our moral agency. Not surprisingly, human beings have sometimes even been described (analogously) as "cocreators" with God. These gifts of material sufficiency and participation in divine providence are actualized through economic life, including market operations.

In sum, Catholic social thought supports markets based on philosophical and theological arguments. Both faith and reason point to markets as part of human nature and as important venues by which God lavishes us with the gifts of material sufficiency and participation in God's providence. Markets are yet once again an illustration of how God works through nature. Grace builds on nature.

THE PROMISE AND RISK OF CHARITY

DAVID HOLLENBACH

Pope Benedict's encyclical, *Caritas in veritate*, begins with several ringing affirmations of the role of charity in shaping the Christian response to urgent social issues that mark our increasingly integrated global society. Arguing that "charity is at the heart of the Church's social doctrine," Benedict sees charity as the source of the virtues of courage and generosity that are needed to sustain Christian "engagement in the field of justice and peace." The encyclical describes charity as a political virtue that works to enhance the quality not only of "micro-relationships (with friends, with family members or within small groups) but also macro-relationships (social, economic, and political ones)" (*CV*, 2). It affirms that this political form of charity is just as fully Christian as that form that serves the neighbor in direct encounters of service (*CV*, 70).

The encyclical makes strong claims that charity is a norm appropriate to the public life of our contemporary pluralistic world by arguing that it is an "authentic expression of humanity" (*CV*, 3). Charity encourages us to promote the deepest requirements of human nature and our true humanity. Action shaped by charity will also lead to the realization of the common good of a truly human society. The requirements of charity, therefore, include respect for human nature as discovered through the authentic use of human reason. Therefore those who are not Christian should also be able to recognize the important role of charity in public life.

At the same time, the encyclical argues that the deepest meaning of charity can only be known from the standpoint of Christian faith, which enables us to see God's love for us as gratuitous and beyond anything we deserve. It is, first of all, "creative love," a love that led God freely and graciously to create the world, the human race, and each individual human being. It is "redemptive love," through which sinful human beings have been re-created in Christ and the Holy Spirit. Charity understood in this light is above all a form of love that freely and graciously gives—God giving us being through our creation, and giving us new being through forgiveness and re-creation. The encyclical repeatedly describes charity as gift, as grace, and as gratuitous. There can be no doubt, therefore, that Benedict's social thought begins from and remains deeply rooted in the creative and redeeming love God has for human beings in and through Jesus Christ.

Starting from this theological understanding of charity as seen in God's love for humanity, the pope moves on to a consideration of the ethical implications of charity for social, economic, and political life. Accepting the gift of God gratuitously given in Jesus Christ empowers humans to become authentically open to their brothers and sisters and thus capable of working effectively for the solidarity so sorely needed in our world (*CV*, 78). The encyclical speaks of how the experience of the gratuitous love of God leads men and women to give the gift of love to others. This gift creates bonds of fraternity and solidarity. Achieving these bonds of unity will go beyond the demands of justice in market exchanges and even beyond what reason tells us is required by our humanity (*CV*, 6, 19). Though justice is presupposed by love, charity as gratuitous concern for one's neighbor transcends justice and makes it possible.

Love as gracious, even undeserved, giving is surely one way that humans can imitate the love God has for them in their interpersonal and social relations with each other. Perhaps the fullest expressions of charity as gift are the forgiveness that a person or community offers to another who has oppressed them, or the self-sacrifice that leads one person or community to surrender its own well-being on behalf another. Such forgiveness has, of course, become newly salient in political life through recent movements for reconciliation based on the model of the Truth and Reconciliation Commission in South Africa.

This emphasis on how charity-as-gift can contribute to solidarity today is surely important. Clearly we need moral and spiritual forces that go beyond the pursuit of narrowly defined self-interest within the global economy. However, the encyclical's interpretation of charity as a gratuitous gift is not the only possible interpretation of its meaning, and linking charity with gift in an almost exclusive way carries some significant dangers. An understanding of charity that includes other important dimensions of Christian love can counteract these dangers.

There is a serious risk if Christian love is seen preeminently as a form of self-gift or self-sacrifice that transcends the requirements of justice, especially if this transcendence is interpreted to mean that love could call for surrender to injustice. Christian love does not require the issuing of a blank check that leads to submission to exploitation.[18] Indeed, Christian love may call for self-defense in some circumstances. Nor does Christian love call for one to stand aside when one's neighbor is being exploited. Love for an innocent neighbor can call one to come to her defense if she is being violated.

Charity understood as gratuitous self-gift or self-sacrifice, therefore, needs to be complemented by an understanding that sees that we are called to love our neighbors with equal regard. Each and every neighbor is irreducibly valuable and is to be treated as such, independent of their special characteristics. This form of love reflects the fact that each person has been created in the image of God and is loved by God in Christ. This dimension of Christian love overlaps in very important ways with justice understood as respect for the equality of all persons.

When Christian love is understood this way, it requires justice and comes to expression in the pursuit of justice. *Caritas in veritate* affirms the link of charity to justice when it states that "justice is inseparable from charity" (*CV*, 6). In the encyclical, however, this affirmation of the link between charity and justice is preceded by the statement that "charity transcends justice and completes it in the logic of giving and forgiving" (*CV*, 6). The precedence granted to charity over justice risks demoting the work of justice to a lower spiritual plane than the love-as-gift that the encyclical strongly and repeatedly stresses.

In addition, Christian love can also be a positive, reciprocal relation like the mutual concern that exists among friends—love as mutuality or solidarity. The encyclical points to this form of love when it describes charity as a form of communion. Significantly, it adds that such communion can and should exist within public life, including its economic sectors. This will happen when solidarity among the members of society builds the common good (*CV*, 36). In order for the unity that can be achieved in social life to be a genuine form of solidarity, it must be fully reciprocal. And this reciprocity requires equality. Charity as a gratuitous gift, however, calls neither for the equality nor the reciprocity that is essential to solidarity. Indeed, it risks seeing charity as a stance taken by a superior or more powerful donor to a subordinate or weaker recipient.

Since love as mutuality requires equality and reciprocity, we need to ask whether the encyclical's interpretation of love-as-gift will support the social and structural innovations required in a world marked by steep inequalities in both power and wealth. The encyclical clearly wants to affirm the importance of the structural changes needed for development. But in stressing that charity "transcends every law of justice" (*CV*, 34) and by failing to carefully consider the way Christian love calls for both equal regard and reciprocal mutuality, it downplays those aspects of love that are most important in the quest for structural change. One can also ask, therefore, whether the encyclical's approach to the relation of love and justice is consistent, and whether its approach is adequate for addressing key practical matters on the development agenda today, including the alleviation of poverty in developing countries. A fully adequate theological grounding for Catholic social teaching requires, then, an appreciation of love as gratuity and an awareness that gratuity alone is both inadequate to the task of institutional change and only part of what the Catholic tradition has to say about the moral life.

LISTENING TO THE EXPERIENCE OF THE POOR

JOHAN VERSTRAETEN

In *Caritas in veritate,* Pope Benedict eloquently laments the tendency of the prosperous to ignore the poor:

> Insignificant matters are considered shocking, yet unprecedented injustices seem to be widely tolerated. While the poor of the world continue knocking on the doors of the rich, the world of affluence runs the risk of no longer hearing those knocks, on account of a conscience that can no longer distinguish what is human. (*CV,* 75)

The dangerous memory of the suffering of Christ urges us to see with new eyes and to look at the achievements of markets or political powers from the perspective of the poor. The preferential option for the poor—now adopted by papal social thought from liberation theology—is in this regard not simply a Christian commitment. It has also an objective dimension, since it enables us to judge economic decisions in the light of how they affect the quality of life of the poor and to assess lifestyles, policies, and social institutions in terms of their impact on the poor. We should not forget, as the French suggest, that society has the face of its victims. This face is real.

The presence of the poor as the real suffering victims of history has a theological meaning.

> Among all the signs we see in every age—some of them obvious and some barely perceptible—there is always one that stands out, in the light of which we can discern and interpret all the others. That sign is the face of crucified people, always present in every century, although the historical method of crucifixion constantly changes. This crucified people is the historical successor of the

> lowly servant of Yahweh, still deprived of human form by the sin of the world.[19]

In our age, these historically crucified people are still present: the thousands of women raped in East Congo, the abused home workers serving the prosperous, the millions of economic migrants who work in inhuman circumstances, the undocumented migrants rejected in Europe and the United States, indigenous people driven off their land to facilitate mining or oil extraction, citizens overburdened by debts, people losing their pensions as a consequence of the banking crisis.

As Filipino theologian Rolando Tuazon affirms, we must learn to see the face of Christ in the visage of suffering humanity. We must recognize how the exclusion of the poor manifests the sinfulness of the systems of which they are the victims, the implication of which is that it is not sufficient to focus on individual responsibility. We must learn that "their struggle for life, truth, justice and peace becomes concrete manifestations of God's in-breaking into human history." According to Tuazon, the excluded and oppressed "other" enjoys an "epistemic privilege in allowing the in-breaking of the Kingdom of God into our history."[20] If that is true, their perspective must be adopted in the (re)interpretation of our social tradition. From the perspective of the poor, any artificial separation of love and justice becomes completely unacceptable,[21] and in this regard *Caritas in veritate* is a step forward because it points to the institutional dimension of the problem of hunger:

> Hunger is not so much dependent on lack of material things as on shortage of social resources, the most important of which are institutional. What is missing in other words is a network of economic institutions capable of guaranteeing regular access to sufficient food and water for nutritional needs. The problem of food insecurity needs to be addressed within a long-term perspective, eliminating the structural causes that give rise to it and promoting the agricultural development of poorer countries. (*CV*, 27)

Our challenge is to revisit the words of the now-marginalised 1971 document *Justitia in mundo* in which the bishops once proclaimed that "action on behalf of justice and *participation in the transformation of the* World" is "a constitutive dimension of the preaching of the Gospel, or, in other words, of the Church's mission for the redemption of the human race and its liberation from every oppressive situation."[22] If we are faithful to the suffering of Christ, the Christian community can become such a transformative power in the history of humankind.

As Pope Benedict has said, humanity can "shape the earthly city in unity and peace, rendering it to some degree anticipation and a prefiguration of the undivided city of God" (*CV*, 9), but this will only occur with the real participation of the poor.

Chapter 3

Markets and Government

> Economic life undoubtedly requires contracts, in order to regulate relations of exchange between goods of equivalent value. But it also needs just laws and forms of redistribution governed by politics, and what is more, it needs works redolent of the spirit of gift.
>
> —Benedict XVI, *Caritas in veritate,* 37

Pope Benedict follows the lead of Pope John Paul II in his insistence that neither market nor government should be allowed to dominate the other. In fact, both require the presence of gratuity and reciprocity, something we engage in the next two chapters.

An approach to Benedict's contributions to the ongoing debates about the relation of markets and government needs to consider the vitality and productivity of markets as well as the realities of market failure. Similarly needed is a view of the role of government in providing the juridical framework for markets and the role of individual morality in any successful creation and enforcement of law. And in our globalized economy today, the pope's call for an international authority capable of providing such a juridical framework across the planet grows in importance each year. The diversity of perspectives and disciplines represented by the authors in this chapter provides a robust examination of Pope Benedict's approach to the relation of markets and government, even though the change in lens of analysis from one text to the other requires of the reader a willingness to see common problems from multiple perspectives in sequence.

THE VITALITY OF MARKETS

MICHAEL NOVAK

Pope Benedict's stress on the role of *caritas* in moral life is a refreshing return to the fundamentals of Catholic faith. Unfortunately, some readers have leapt from *caritas* to the old error of viewing contemporary economic life as particularly subject to greed.

Greed is universal, and present in every age, often in virulent form. Max Weber, the great sociologist of the economy, once presented arguments to show that capitalism is of all human economic systems the least supportive of greed, not the most. One reason is that it offers rich successful men the chance to put all their money at risk again, in order to invest in new ventures. Capitalists do not hoard their wealth. They invest it. And these investments create whole new industries, new technologies, new jobs, and new wealth.

Not many years ago, an apparently poor lady of very advanced age was found dead in her Louisiana home. In the closets around her, in her cupboards and in the drawers of her dressers, were scores of certificates of ownership for stocks and bonds. It turned out that on paper this woman was extremely rich. Yet finding these certificates, witnesses did not think of this poor woman as a Midas, a miser, greedy and grasping. No, they thought of her as a bit crazy because she did not reinvest these papers and turn them to creative purposes. Capitalism has made the miser obsolete.

Capitalistic systems produce more new wealth for their own method of redistribution than any other known system. They raise up the poor in prodigal numbers: over half a billion human beings in China and India during just the last thirty years have left behind a poverty that has existed for millenia. Indeed, the United States was an undeveloped country less than 200 years ago, until its choice in favor of building a commercial republic (instead of an aristocratic republic) got going in earnest.

The benefits for the poor achieved through the spread of economic enterprise and markets (capitalism is for some too unpleasant a word to use) should be more resoundingly attended to. In 1970, for instance, the life expectancy of men and women in Bangladesh was 44.6 years, but by

2005 it had risen to 63. Think what a joy and what vigor such increased longevity means to individual families.

Similarly, the infant mortality rate in Bangladesh in 1970 was 15.2 percent. By 2005 this average had been brought down to a little less than 6 percent. Again, what pain this lifts from ordinary mothers and fathers, and what joy it brings. There is surely more to do to raise health standards for Bangladesh, but the progress just in this past thirty years is unprecedented in world history.

Famines were once endemic every twenty years or so in many major cities of the world. Wherever capitalism has arisen, such famines have disappeared. Similarly, plagues and widespread epidemics have been in some cases eliminated, in others tamed, and in virtually all cases it was new vaccinations and other preventive methods that soon contained them. As Pope John Paul II put it in *Centesimus annus,* what makes capitalism capitalism is its inventiveness, its creativity, its know-how (*CA*, 32).

BENEFITS OF MARKETS

ALBINO BARRERA

Much of the debate among Christians about economic life has been carried out by people at the opposite ends of the political spectrum: neoconservatives who only sing the praises of capitalism and liberationists who only decry its abuses. Given the call of Pope Benedict in *Caritas in veritate* for us to enter such debates with charity and truth, a more balanced account of both assets and debits of markets is necessary. This short essay reviews ten positive features of the set of economic arrangements we call a market.

There is no doubt that government action is necessary not only to correct market failures but also to ensure the smooth functioning of markets (consider the 2008 global financial meltdown). Nevertheless, such extramarket oversight must be conducted with great care, so it can channel the market's vitality to produce its manifold benefits without dissipating the energy that produces them.

First, no other social institution can yet match the market's allocative efficiency, that is, its ability to supply the right goods and services in the right quantities and quality, at the right place, at the right time, and at the right price, and to accomplish all these with the right methods and inputs. The price mechanism makes this massive and complex orchestration possible because market prices continuously convey enormous amounts of information to geographically dispersed economic agents in a cost-efficient manner. In fact, price changes are the catalysts that push market participants to adjust their choices and reallocate their resources in light of shifting economic conditions.

Second, markets provide an expansive sphere of autonomy because they operate on the assumption that people know and pursue what is in their own best interest. Private initiative is the warp and woof of market activity. Consequently, more than at any time in history, people enjoy extensive geographic and socioeconomic mobility, thanks in no small part to the wide liberties made possible by the modern marketplace.

Third, by affording individual economic agents broad freedom of action, markets reinforce their own capacity to create value. In contrast to the premodern economy of precarious subsistence, the accumulation of surplus is the norm today. The modern economy supports the largest population base ever, and at a much higher per capita income. Luxury goods and services that were once reserved for the very wealthy have become items of mass consumption (e.g., travel and retirement).

Fourth, markets are incubators of ceaseless innovations. Joseph Schumpeter famously characterized capitalism as creative destruction. Markets unleash enormous energy and ingenuity because they provide economic agents with both the freedom and the pecuniary incentives for risk taking. Moreover, the unforgiving and unrelenting nature of market competition leaves no room for complacency. Consequently, market participants are forward looking in anticipating the public's needs and in developing ever-new products.

Fifth, markets facilitate the pursuit of unusually speculative or prohibitively expensive projects that would not otherwise have been undertaken. After all, market exchange can spread risks (e.g., derivatives) and raise enormous sums of capital (e.g., the securities industry). Markets provide the venue for collaborative work in inherently risky but socially useful endeavors (e.g., oil prospecting, commercial space exploration, drug development) that otherwise would not have been pursued.

Sixth, markets contribute to stability in the face of chance and the contingencies of life. While speculative trading can precipitate wild market gyrations (recall the dotcom and housing bubbles), it can nonetheless also dampen the amplitude of business cycles, if conducted responsibly. Speculators mop up excess supplies (and thereby prevent a further drop in prices) and then sell their inventories in times of excess demand (and thereby prevent a further increase in prices). Arbitrage promotes greater market efficiency by minimizing the over- or underpricing of goods or services caused by information asymmetries.

Seventh, markets can instill both personal and collective discipline and virtue. For the most part, market participants have to internalize the costs and benefits of their economic decisions in order to do well; they are compelled to behave accordingly. Thus, shopkeepers work hard, provide quality goods, are honest in furnishing services, and take an interest in the lives of their clients, if only out of self-interest in wanting to have loyal customers. Conscientious brand-name owners, such as Nike and Gap, carefully vet their subcontractors in other nations for fear of being associated with sweatshops and losing the public goodwill that they have carefully nurtured over the years at great expense.

Eighth, markets provide mechanisms that cut down waste and the unsustainable use of natural resources. For example, when oil peaked at nearly $150 per barrel in 2008, people voluntarily changed their wasteful habits and found creative ways of economizing on energy usage. Trading in carbon emissions is a cost-effective way of slowing down global warming. African villagers took an active role in fighting elephant poaching after getting a share of the tourist revenues generated by elephant herds. Fishermen restrain their annual hauls and patrol at-risk fishing grounds once they are given exclusive fishing rights. People take an active interest in protecting the ecology if they have a pecuniary stake in doing so, and markets are essential in providing such incentives.

Ninth, even as governments redress market failures, the market, in its own turn, can also correct government shortcomings. In particular, markets often step in whenever governments fail to provide essential public goods. Thus, privately funded, built, and operated toll roads are common in many countries because of a dearth of public funds, political will, or expertise. In some developing countries, such privatization extends to the provision of even the most basic and essential goods, such as water, particularly in nations where corruption hobbled such provision by government agencies. In the United States, local and federal governments increasingly resort to markets and outsource the management of charter schools, public libraries, prisons, and even entire school systems.

Tenth, markets allow for the orderly intergenerational and interpersonal lending of resources. Market exchange permits the smoothing of consumption and earnings across a person's lifetime. For example, the young incur student loans (borrowed against their potential future earnings) as they build their human capital through education early in life. They take out home mortgages as they start their own families. The middle-aged earn, save, and invest to pay down their student loans and house mortgages, even while building a nest egg for their retirement. As retirees, they draw down their savings accumulated during their productive years. Capital markets make possible this smoothing of consumption and earnings over a person's lifetime.

Of course, for all the benefits of markets we must also consider their well-known deficiencies and ill effects. There is a proper role for both the market and government in socioeconomic life. In fact, they are necessary complements to each other. The key is to strike a balance between the two. Like the other modern Catholic social documents, *Caritas in veritate* affirms both the value of markets and their limitations.

GOVERNMENT AND JURIDICAL FRAMEWORK

J. BRYAN HEHIR

Caritas in vertitate explicitly endorses the framework established in Catholic teaching by John Paul II in *Centesimus annus*. More explicitly than any of his predecessors, John Paul II acknowledged the significance of the market in the modern economy. He also argued that the market required an encompassing "juridical framework" if it was to be an instrument of social justice as well as a source of wealth.

In his assessment of state, market, and civil society, Pope Benedict asserts that "wisdom and prudence suggest not being too precipitous in declaring the demise of the state" (*CV*, 41), an important statement if we are to assess *Caritas in veritate* in light of the U.S. case. It highlights in Catholic teaching what might be called the moral role of government in the modern economy.

The debate about social policy in the United States today involves much dismissing or denigrating of the role of government. Politicians run against government; the public is at least ambivalent (with some groups virulently critical); and policy debates are intensely divided about the appropriate size and role of the government. Catholic teaching has a useful contribution to make. The substance of the teaching is traditional; its application to the United States at this time could be distinctive, promoting a civil conversation on the role of the state in the economic order.

Essentially, the Church's teaching affirms the moral duties of the state and a positive role for government in economic matters. Clearly, the teaching is not statist; that is to say, it does not see the state as the major actor in the economy. The principle of subsidiarity is described by Benedict as "a particular manifestation of charity" and "an effective antidote against any form of all-encompassing welfare state," and is a baseline for assessing the nature and role of the state (*CV*, 57). Subsidiarity is complemented by the Church's understanding of its own role in society. In multiple cultures and settings, the Church creates institutions—schools, health care, and social service agencies—that work in collaboration with the state, but that also provide for a pluralist structure of power in society.

John Paul II described a double function for the state in *Centesimus annus*, directed by the twin principles of subsidiarity and solidarity. Subsidiarity identifies an indirect role for the state in society: "creating favorable conditions for the free exercise of economic activity." Solidarity identifies the direct role of the state: "defending the weak by placing certain limits on the autonomy of the parties who determine working conditions, and by ensuring in every case the necessary minimum support for the unemployed worker" (*CA*, 15). The intersection of these two criteria defines a role for a limited but activist state in the economic order. *Caritas in veritate* does not expand upon this direct/indirect framework for the state, but its address to the economic crisis of the last three years invokes John Paul II's model in its call for legal and political restraints in the financial sector and for a systemic response to assist those harmed by unemployment and stagnant economies.

Simply by insisting on traditional Catholic teaching on the role of government in society, *Caritas in veritate* and its immediate predecessors (reaching back to *Mater et magistra*) can provide an antidote to the sometimes venomous contemporary policy debate on the short- and long-term role of the government in the economic order. Much of the debate is unfortunately cast in terms of the size of government, as if one would choose a car or a pair of shoes based on size alone. A Catholic approach focuses on the nature of the state and the moral responsibility of government that flows from it. Catholic social thought insists that the role of the state includes a moral dimension and must be exercised in collaboration with other actors, not overwhelming them.

MARKET FAILURE AND THE ROLE OF GOVERNMENT

REBECCA M. BLANK

Markets can be a powerful force for economic development and wealth creation. But the operation of markets does not always result in a socially optimal outcome. Any Christian moral assessment of economic life must engage both the benefits and harms markets can cause, something Pope Benedict is deeply aware of in *Caritas in veritate*. Yet even economists, who often define development much more narrowly than the pope, are generally in agreement that market failure can and does occur (i.e., market outcomes do not always produce the best economic result). There is, however, deep disagreement within the economics community about how frequently market failure occurs.

Most economists think about market failure solely as defined in standard economic theory, what might be called *traditional market failure*. This includes situations where full information is not available to both parties in an economic transaction; where economic transactions result in costs or benefits to third parties who are not part of the economic transaction (often referred to as *market externalities*); or where public goods are present that can be widely used by many people, including persons who did not purchase them. In all of these situations, the standard price-setting mechanism in the market does not work effectively and market solutions need to be "corrected" with regulations that lead to better market outcomes.

But two other broad forms of market failure can also occur. In some cases, market outcomes are not considered acceptable, not because the market malfunctions but because it results in a set of outcomes that cause serious economic or social disadvantage, often because there are individuals who cannot participate effectively in the market. This might be called *market inadequacy*. For instance, there may be a need to supplement incomes among individuals who cannot earn an adequate income due to age or disability or skill level, or to provide health insurance to those who are unable to afford it in the market. In this case, government or private-sector programs often respond by redistributing income to those whose needs are not met by the market.

A third type of market failure occurs in situations where market-based activity (buying and selling, at a level determined by price) is inappropriate. Call this *market inappropriateness*. There are large areas of our civic life that we explicitly place outside of markets. This occurs where we do not allow buying or selling or do not recognize price as a legitimate basis on which to provide access to these goods. For example, we do not allow persons to buy or sell juror votes, police protection, or court convictions and sentencing. When these occur, they are evidence of corruption. With some exceptions, we do not allow people to sell their bodies or body parts. Many internal family decisions are placed apart from the market, so families cannot buy or sell children, while spouses take oaths to support each other in good times and bad—that is, regardless of the price of such support.

Similarly, Christian theology insists that grace is one of those aspects of life for which market-based thinking is inappropriate. Grace is undeserved and ever-present (*CV*, 5). Access to God's kingdom cannot be bought or sold with earthly wealth; churches reflect this by welcoming everyone to worship and to communion as free-of-charge activities, where all are served in the same manner. While there is a cost to Christian discipleship, it is not measured in market terms.

Markets can be a force for good; indeed, the spread of successful markets in the developing world is a primary reason for widespread reductions in global poverty. But markets can also be destructive. Economic growth can bring new opportunities for increased income and for the application of human ingenuity to existing problems, but it can also cause displacement and the erosion of communities. In most cases, economic change brings both good and bad at the same time. Globalization, innovation, and marketization are a source of good outcomes for some and of increased insecurity and economic difficulties for others. Our response to these issues as individuals and as a society must be based on a framework that allows us to discern both the good and the bad. Rather than rejecting economic change because it has negative effects, the goal should be to seek ways to limit and mitigate the negative effects.

Government responds to traditional market failures through regulations that offset market problems. For instance, the public sector can demand full disclosure of information by businesses to buyers; it can regulate pollution emissions in response to negative externalities; and it typically provides public goods such as national defense or highways, thereby resolving the difficulties of providing public goods through the private market.

In response to market inadequacy, government "rearranges" private market outcomes through redistributional programs. Resources are redistributed to lower-income families, to elderly individuals, and to those who are unemployed (and, unfortunately, to groups that are simply well-organized politically). Of course, other civic organizations, and particularly the Church, are often actively involved in redistributional activities, a type of charity to which all Christians are called (*CV*, 27).

In cases of market inappropriateness, government is the primary enforcer of rules that protect certain domains of activity from markets. Laws are established that make it illegal to engage in market transactions in those areas where market mechanisms are considered unethical methods of decision making.

By itself, government is inadequate at enforcing these restraints on the market and its outcomes unless the public is in broad agreement. This emphasizes the important role of the teachings of churches and other religious bodies in shaping citizen beliefs. In the long run, laws are effective (i.e., durable and enforceable) only when they regulate behavior in ways that are considered appropriate by the citizenry. Laws against corruption have little impact in a culture where bribery is considered the normal way of doing business. Laws against prostitution have limited effects when a significant number of buyers and sellers want to exchange sex for money. Political debates over redistributional programs in the United States have always emphasized the need to help only those who are "deserving" of public assistance; those who are considered undeserving do not receive public assistance.

These examples illustrate that it is not entirely accurate to claim that government is an independent actor responsible for regulating markets and their outcomes. While the government can enact regulations and laws that address various types of market failure, in a society with individual freedoms, these limitations on the market will work effectively only if they are supported by the citizenry. This requires a consensus among the citizens about which instances of market failure require regulation, redistribution, or the outright banning of particular market behavior. That is, ethical deliberation is critical to devising effective ways to prevent the damage market failures cause. *Caritas in veritate* calls for exactly this sort of deliberation by Christians interested in applying Christian principles to economic life.

INSTITUTIONS AND INDIVIDUAL MORALITY

REBECCA M. BLANK

A common framework of ethical beliefs about right and wrong action on the part of citizens can assist in the smooth functioning of a democratic system. This is true for markets as well, as was noted by Adam Smith, the father of modern economics, as well as by Pope Benedict (*CV*, 45). Broad agreement on right behavior within the market is necessary for smooth market operations, since monitoring and legal enforcement of rules is expensive and can only be called upon occasionally in cases of repeated or egregious violations.

But it is not enough to rely on individuals, acting by themselves, to behave in a consistently ethical manner. Individuals often cannot or do not want to see the implications of their decisions. They are often swayed by short-term considerations and by personal interest. Individuals are typically guided by the environment around them; for instance, they will be more corrupt in an environment that allows or even encourages corruption.

A society needs effectively functioning institutions to help channel and guide individual behavior. This involves public agencies that monitor and enforce laws—courts or regulatory agencies—to ensure that an evenhanded set of rules is enforced and applies to all citizens. But enforcement agencies are only a small part of the institutional structure of a society. Private sector institutions can encourage better or worse behavior by creating a set of social norms about how management and workers behave and treat each other, about employee responsibility for high-quality work and good customer relations, or about cooperation with external regulators. Public sector institutions that function effectively and treat taxpayers and clients with respect are more likely to generate cooperation and support for public activities. The Church plays a key role in providing a community of practice and of teaching that supports ethical behavior.

Pope Benedict understands this (*CV*, 40) but a common gap in much theological writing about economics and markets (including much of the discussion in *Caritas in veritate*) is that it focuses too little attention on the importance of institutions and the ways in which institutions might be structured to reinforce and encourage "right behavior." This is as true for church organizations as for market-based firms and government agencies.

GLOBALIZATION AND GLOBAL GOVERNANCE

J. BRYAN HEHIR

Since Pope John XXIII's 1961 encyclical *Mater et Magistra*, Catholic social teaching has focused on the growing interdependence of states, nations, and populations—an interdependence most vivid in political economy, but also in politics, culture, science, and law. By the 1990s, the scope and intensity of interdependence called forth the idea of globalization, again with primary reference to political economy but with increasing relevance to international politics as a whole. John Paul II introduced the term *globalization* into the social teaching and Benedict addresses it in *Caritas in veritate* when he speaks of the unrelenting growth of global interdependence.

The lines of continuity in *Caritas in veritate* with earlier papal teaching are evident in two ways. First, like John Paul II, Benedict rejects any sense that globalization is a deterministic material process beyond human control. In a decisive quote from *Centesimus annus,* Benedict reiterates that "globalization, a priori, is neither good nor bad. It will be what people make of it." Benedict then immediately adds his basic judgment: "We should not be its victims but its protagonists, acting in the light of reason, guided by charity and truth" (*CV,* 42). Second, Pope Benedict pursues the theme of human direction of globalization by returning to John XXIII's call in *Pacem in terris* for a universal political authority to assist a world of growing interdependence governed by independent states.

Globalization is one of those topics in *Caritas in veritate* that calls for deeper empirical development and greater moral direction. A more detailed description of the multiple agents of globalization, greater attention to the differing capacities of states and peoples to address it, and particular attention to the challenges posed by liberalized financial flows and capital markets is needed. Benedict's call for "a true world political authority" echoes that of John XXIII. However, Pope John's focus was primarily on issues of war, peace, and human rights, while Pope Benedict makes this appeal against the background of a deep global economic crisis. But the intervening decades have seen dramatic changes in the arena of international political economy. The role of a global political authority in directing these institutions is different from and arguably more difficult—economically and ethically—than the challenges faced in John XXIII's day. Benedict's call for such an authority met resistance in financial quarters, but even those in support of his proposal must recognize that balancing the dynamics of freedom and intervention in trade, finance, and investment is a more delicate task than addressing the role of sovereign states in the arenas of war and human rights.

Finding the right balance of market freedoms and government's juridical framework is difficult in a nation as large and complicated as the United States. Accomplishing a similar feat on the global stage will be even more so.

FROM GOVERNMENT TO GOVERNANCE

JOHN A. COLEMAN

Pope Benedict clearly recognizes the promises and problems generated by globalization, and this awareness lies below his call for an effective means to "manage the global economy" (*CV*, 67). Such management is essential in providing the needed juridical framework for so much economic activity that transcends national boundaries and laws. Yet the pope's proposal lacks imagination in dealing with the dilemma of global governance.

On the one hand, Benedict's proposal does endorse subsidiarity. Its argument, effectively, runs: large global institutions are needed to promote global solutions to global problems. Their power should rest at the bottom, not the top. They should be held to transparency and accountability. These institutions should be guided morally. Effectively, a plea is then made for the reform of the United Nations, the International Monetary Fund, and the World Bank. But this plea for reform of the international organizations is not accompanied by any inquiry into why such long-sought reform has not occurred (others have been making this plea for fifty years now). Is it merely because the political will is lacking? Is it because these organizations have become too broken to fix? Is it, in fact, too much to expect these bureaucratic organizations to operate in this way?

Questions about global government are better understood as questions of global governance. Of course, truly global problems need truly global solutions that are feasible and effective. Institutional infrastructure is needed for global governance. But much of global governance is not done by states or international governmental institutions such as the United Nations, but by regimes and global policy networks.

Some global governance regimes are purely state centered and controlled through a standing intergovernmental organization, such as the World Trade Organization, or through multilateral treaties. Some regimes, such as the World Bank, are state centered but with specific provisions for private sector access, input, and voice. Some, such as the Basle Committee on Banking Regulation and Supervisory Practices, involve public-private partnerships between, for example, international governmental organizations and banks. Finally, some global regimes, such as the Internet Corporation for Assigned Names, are purely private. The International Chemical Association drew up its own codes to regulate chemical pollution. Standard and Poor's rates bonds internationally.

Global policy networks involve flexible public-private and frequently time-bound concatenations of nongovernmental organizations, intergovernmental organizations, and multinational corporations. There are literally hundreds of functioning global policy networks, including the International Campaign to Ban Landmines, which could bypass the United Nations (and the powerful U.S. veto in the UN Security Council) to bring about a new regime, anchored in a multilateral treaty. Other examples include the World Commission on Dams (which unites intergovernmental organizations like the World Bank, corporations, governments and environmental nongovernmental organizations), the International Coalition to Stop the Use of Child Soldiers, and Transparency International (which focuses on exposing and reducing corruption in governments and corporations). We are, increasingly, living in a networked world following a logic of networks and providing governance through such networks. This is closer to the subsidiarity Catholic thought endorses.

To become more effective and credible in globalization debates, Catholic social thought needs to pay more attention to multiple global governance forms and the ethical criteria needed to judge these institutions. Catholic social teaching talks little about regimes and global policy networks. But the lofty and often vague talk about a global common good demands more than attention to the United Nations and other international governmental organizations.[1] In sum, official Catholic social thought seems overly fixated on governments and government-controlled institutions and not attentive enough to alternative forms of global governance. These alternative forms of governance are becoming more and more important in providing an ethically based framework for global life, a fundamental recommendation of *Caritas in veritate*.

Chapter 4

Reconceiving "Relation"

Relationships between human beings throughout history cannot but be enriched by reference to this divine model. In particular, in the light of the revealed mystery of the Trinity, we understand that true openness does not mean loss of individual identity but profound interpenetration.

—Benedict XVI, *Caritas in veritate*, 54

Because of the relational character of our Trinitarian God, Christians are continually challenged to better conceive of and more thoroughly embody the relatedness of persons that God's call has insisted upon from biblical times to the present. Pope Benedict's *Caritas in veritate* distinguishes itself in the eloquence of its call for rethinking our understanding of "relation," not simply in our interpersonal lives but within economic life and structures.

Particularly important here is careful attention to the theological understanding of relation and in particular of receptivity, as essential to relationships of integrity, which are too often idealistically described as acts of giving only. In trying to bring about social change informed by these basic features of relationships, an understanding of the role of culture in forming the context for relation is critical. The diverse disciplinary perspectives that authors in this chapter bring to this notion of a new paradigm for relation in economic life provide a rich if challenging articulation of many of its contours.

THEOLOGICAL FOUNDATIONS OF HUMAN RELATION

MIGUEL H. DIAZ

Christian thinkers have often turned to the principle of interdependence as a way to describe how creaturely life mirrors divine life. Whether one explores the contribution of classical voices (e.g., the Cappadocian Fathers, Irenaeus, Augustine, Bonaventure, or Thomas Aquinas) or more contemporary voices (e.g., Balthasar, Barth, Rahner, LaCugna, Pannenberg, Boff, Johnson, or Zizioulas), the principle of interdependence is central to describing life in the image of the Christian God. In Christian tradition the principle of interdependence is a signpost (though not a blueprint) that carries numerous personal, communal, and sociopolitical implications.

Nowhere is this understanding of interdependence exemplified more clearly than in the social doctrine of the Church. In *Sollicitudo rei socialis,* Pope John Paul II emphasized the increasing interdependence of the human family, relating this interdependence to the Christian doctrine of God and pointing out some of its contemporary sociopolitical implications. As the *Compendium of the Social Doctrine of the Church* puts it,

> The commandment of mutual love, which represents the law of life for God's people, must inspire, purify, and elevate all human relationships in society and in politics. "To be human means to be called to interpersonal communion," because the image and the likeness of the Trinitarian God are the basis of the whole of "human 'ethos,' which reaches its apex in the commandment of love." The modern cultural, social, economic, and political phenomenon of interdependence, which intensifies and makes particularly evident the bonds that unite the human family, accentuates once more, in the light of Revelation, "a new model of the unity of the human race, which must ultimately inspire our solidarity."[1]

Echoing Thomistic ways of relating human actions, knowledge, and love, *Caritas in veritate* declares that "deeds without knowledge are blind, and knowledge without love is sterile" (*CV*, 30).[2] Indeed, one of the central themes of the encyclical is the relation of right thinking (orthodoxy) and right doing (orthopraxis). In this encyclical, the truth given the greater attention is this: human persons are relational and social beings. This truth describes the heart of human nature and finds increased expression today in the interdependence that characterizes the world we live in.

Fittingly titled "The Cooperation of the Human Family," chapter 5 of *Caritas in veritate* contains a rich reflection on what has become a central category of contemporary philosophical and theological reflection: the category of relation.[3] Rejecting isolation, the encyclical embraces relationship to others and interdependence as essential to what it means to be human, and as the signpost for envisioning just and truth-filled economic initiatives. Rooted in the Christian Trinitarian notion of persons in community (*CV*, 54), the encyclical's arguments reflect ongoing Roman Catholic concerns to affirm the relational nature of human and other creaturely existence and to reconcile individual and communal identity. Avoiding both individualism and collectivism, Roman Catholic social teaching has always underscored the particular yet communal nature of persons. Simply put, from a Catholic point of view, to be human is to be *for* and *from* others.

Closely related to this fundamental Catholic teaching are the principles of subsidiarity and solidarity. The principle of subsidiarity defines the relationship between levels of governance, from neighborhood and city to individual nation-states and worldwide public authorities. It protects the rights that individuals and families have before the state. The principle affirms that the state exists for the well-being of individuals (not vice versa) and that nothing should be done by a higher or larger organization that can be done as well by a lower or smaller one. On the other hand, the principle of solidarity affirms the ontological connection within the human species and the basic ethical responsibility to exercise care for one another, especially for those most in need. Solidarity is a principle that invites the commitment to all persons and sectors in society on behalf of the common good. Noting these two important principles in Catholic social teaching, Pope Benedict XVI writes,

> The principle of subsidiarity must remain closely linked to the principle of solidarity and vice versa, since the former without the latter gives way to social privatism, while the latter without the former gives way to paternalistic social assistance that is demeaning to those in need. This general rule must also be taken broadly into consideration when addressing issues concerning international development. (*CV*, 58)

For Pope Benedict, the affirmation that relationality is essential to being human (*CV*, 55) is the cornerstone on which to construct the humanization of the marketplace. References to gratuitousness, self-giving, reciprocity, fraternity, and human solidarity abound. According to this personalist approach, already strongly promoted by John Paul II, this being *for* and *from* others should be translated into economic relationships so as to create what the encyclical terms "an economy of gratuitousness and fraternity" (*CV*, 38). This relational logic, this openness to others, the pope understands, will expand participation within the marketplace, increase true prosperity, foster just laws, and redistribute human and financial resources in more equitable ways. This relational logic is necessary to realize the integral human development that is the goal for both persons and society.

According to *Caritas in veritate,* this relational understanding of reality carries concrete implications for socioeconomic life. In particular, the encyclical appeals to interdependence as a way to advance integral and inclusive human development. While highly skeptical of idealizing any sector of the marketplace, and dismissive of various economic forms of anthropological reductionism, the encyclical calls for concrete economic measures on behalf of the common good and especially on behalf of poor and marginalized persons who increasingly lack active participation in the market. These measures all require an interpersonal and communal praxis of giving to and receiving from others. Calling for recognition of human rights and the exercise of human responsibility that contributes to the common good, the pope identifies several conditions that threaten life and undermine authentic human development: hunger, deprivation, disease, unemployment, abortion, illiteracy, climate change, and food insecurity.

Referring to "the scandal of glaring inequalities," the encyclical maintains that what is needed today is "a market that permits the free operation, in conditions of equal opportunity, of enterprises in pursuit of different institutional ends" (*CV*, 38). Citing Paul VI's *Populorum progressio*, Pope Benedict calls for an expansion, humanization, and state regulation of the market so that "all will be able to give and receive, without one group making progress at the expense of the other" (*CV*, 39). Finally, in what is perhaps one of the most inclusive affirmations of the interdependence of creaturely life, the pope underscores that "projects for integral human development cannot ignore coming generations, but need to be marked by solidarity and inter-generational justice, while taking into account a variety of contexts: ecological, juridical, economic, political and cultural" (*CV*, 28).

RESOURCES FOR RECEPTIVITY TO A TRANSCENDENT VOCATION

AMELIA J. UELMEN

The entire framework of *Caritas in veritate* hinges on an essentially receptive stance: a capacity to receive and adhere to a plan "that is prior to us" (*CV*, 52)—the love that comes from God—and to let this love constitute one's identity, sense of truth, source of freedom (*CV*, 1, 52, 68), and the "transcendent vocation" to human development (*CV*, 16). However, the conviction that we are the sole authors of ourselves, our life, and our society (*CV*, 34) does indeed make it difficult to "let go of subjective opinions and impressions" (*CV*, 4) and can block our access to the dimension of "the astonishing experience of gift" in our lives (*CV*, 34). Further, given the fabric of our pluralistic society, many are not sure that we are going to be able to "come together in the assessment of the value and substance of things" (*CV*, 4).

What resources might help U.S. culture to move beyond a sense of "freedom as self-definition," toward a stance which is more receptive, more open to a metaphysics that is grounded in a transcendent dimension?[4] Robert Bellah and others have suggested that we should mine the traditions of "civic republicanism" and biblical religion because both offer ways to see "the individual in relation to the larger whole, a community and a tradition," and they might be "capable of sustaining genuine individuality and nurturing both public and private life."[5]

Alexis de Tocqueville also appreciated how religion could not only reinforce self-control and maintain moral standards, but also capture a positive and even contemplative vision that can inspire benevolence and self-sacrifice. Christianity teaches, he wrote, "that one ought to do good to those like oneself for love of God. That is a magnificent expression; man penetrates Divine thought by his intelligence; he sees the goal of God is order; he freely associates himself with the great design; and all the while sacrificing his particular interests to the admirable order of all things, he expects no other recompense than the pleasure of contemplating it."[6]

But at this juncture, Charles Taylor warns that it is not enough to recover a language of commitment to the greater whole—because this recovery does not necessarily grapple with the heart of the dilemma within the self: a loss of meaning and a sense of fragmentation. At this point, Taylor issues a tall order: what we need is an access point to sources of meaning outside the self, but expressed in languages that resonate within the self, "the grasping of an order which is inseparably indexed to a personal vision."[7]

In light of Tocqueville's assessment of the social implications of Christianity—"that one ought do good to those like oneself out of love of God"—Taylor's caveat might be expressed like this: in our modern world we no longer assume that we can "penetrate" Divine thought by our "intelligence," or that we will see any sense of "order," much less one that is "magnificent" or part of "the goal of God." Because so much has been thrown into doubt, many do not sense this connection or conviction from inside themselves—the most important point of reference. For this reason, we struggle mightily with defining our "freedom" as somehow caught up in this "great design."

Caritas in veritate may offer a resource that can help us resolve this tension at its deepest level: its metaphysical understanding of "the category of relation" according to the analogy of the Trinity. What work does this model do? In some ways, the dynamic runs parallel to the text of Tocqueville discussed above: development is grounded in contemplation of God's plan—"the inclusion-in-relation of all individuals and peoples within the one community of the human family," as "illuminated" by the "relationship between the Persons of the Trinity within the one divine Substance" (*CV*, 54). The invitation, however, is not only to the contemplation of an "admirable ordering" but also to participate in this same life: "God desires to incorporate us into this reality of communion as well: 'that they may be one even as we are one'" (John 17:22). And we can access it not only through external contemplation but also by analogizing to "common human experiences of love and truth" (*CV*, 54).

In describing the end result of participation in the life of God, the pope's emphasis, in contrast with Tocqueville's, is less on the capacity to "sacrifice" personal interests than on the discovery of interpersonal relations as being, to use Taylor's phrase, a "source of the self." Pope Benedict explains: "As a spiritual being, the human creature is defined through interpersonal relationships. The more authentically he or she lives these relations, the more his or her own personal identity matures. It is not by isolation that man establishes his worth, but by placing himself in relation with others and with God. Hence these relations take on a fundamental importance" (*CV*, 53).

This approach—in which human community does not "absorb" the individual, or "annihilate" human autonomy, in which "true openness does not mean loss of individual identity but profound interpenetration" (*CV*, 54)—is a promising starting point for U.S. discussions on a cultural framework to sustain a vision of "the individual in relation to the larger whole, a community and a tradition."[8] It is especially helpful because it also indicates a way to meet Taylor's important challenge—to find language to express a profound source of meaning from outside the self that nonetheless resonates within the self as a source of identity: "the grasping of an order which is inseparably indexed to a personal vision."[9] When receptivity and adherence to "that which is prior to us" (*CV*, 52)—the life of the Trinity into which we are incorporated—is perceived as an authentic path to personal identity and maturity, it might be exactly the foundation we need to rework our faulty sense of freedom as "self-definition" (*CV*, 70).[10]

Further, the Trinitarian model of *Caritas in veritate*, grounded in a "metaphysical interpretation of the 'humanum' in which relationality is an essential element" (*CV*, 55), critiques not only egocentric self-interest, but also altruism and self-sacrifice—in that both these attitudes are grounded in an assumption that to engage the other and the other's needs and interests is in fundamental tension with our own identity and interests.[11]

Within this framework, the protagonist is the principle of reciprocity that includes an element of self-interest. In the words of Stefano Zamagni, reciprocity involves this recognition: "I need other people in order to discover that it is worth preserving myself, indeed that I flourish."[12] But the individual seeks to flourish not because, to use Tocqueville's phrase, "private interest" is the "only immutable point in the human heart." Rather, it is because of an "ontological relationality": "the human creature is defined through interpersonal relations" (*CV*, 53). The Trinitarian dynamic is an invitation to plant the roots of self-interest near the much deeper running waters of a metaphysics in which relationality is constitutive of human identity and fulfillment (*CV*, 55).

The principle of reciprocity understood in this way cuts through the Gordian knot of disputes over the proper relation between the interests of the self and the interests of others. Zamagni explains:

> Recognizing the other person as an end in himself and recognizing him as the means for my own fulfillment are reunified, which resolves the reductive dichotomy between Kantian morals, which require that we see the others strictly as an end in themselves, and a theory of instrumental rationality, in which others are seen as the means to one's own ends. The good of self-fulfillment is attained when there is reciprocal recognition.[13]

This foundational dynamic can then in turn become the driver for a societal commitment to the common good. As Zamagni notes: "The original structure of the principle of reciprocity is ternary (I, you, the third). . . . As Paul Ricoeur reminds us, it is the entry of the third into intersubjective relationships that creates society and keeps it alive."[14]

CULTURE AS THE LOCUS FOR ECONOMIC RELATION

MARY L. HIRSCHFELD

So much of contemporary thinking about the economy is founded on how the discipline of economics understands economic life, a conception of human interaction that leaves far too much out of the picture. In *Caritas in veritate,* Pope Benedict argues that we should carve out space for "civil economy" or "civil society" in our analysis of economic matters. As many commentators have observed, the section on the civil economy can seem disjointed from the sections that precede it, but can be read as an attempt to flesh out the difference between an economic setting conducive to integral human development and the economic setting described by economists.

According to *Caritas in veritate,* the standard view of the economy identifies the market as the institution in which we exercise the logic of exchange in a manner that is subject to the principles of commutative justice. However, because the market cannot achieve distributive justice on its own, the political sphere must play a role in pursuing economic justice through redistribution (*CV,* 37). In the market we give in order to acquire, while in the political realm we give as an exercise in duty (*CV,* 39). Giving to acquire—the logic of exchange—is the fundamental language of economics. Individuals pursue their self-interest in markets, which typically results in "efficient" outcomes.

However, markets can fail, and in such cases government intervention can improve market outcomes, hence the focus on policy questions. The two questions that underlie almost all economic policy analysis are: In what cases should the government intervene? And what form should that intervention take?

Pope Benedict argues that this standard economic analysis neglects the importance of the sphere of culture. Consideration of the institutions of the market and the government is insufficient, because institutions are merely instruments. The outcomes that they generate depend crucially on how human agents operate within them. How well markets or governments function depends on the virtues individuals bring to them. For markets to function well there needs to be an environment of mutual trust and reciprocity.

Consider a counterexample. Several corporations have instituted policies designed to squeeze extra cash out of unsuspecting customers. Some banks employ hidden fees to generate income, and several major communications corporations employ bait and switch programs where consumers are often encouraged to sign up for services at low introductory rates to disguise the higher actual cost of the service going forward. Generating such policies is a corporate culture that has an adversarial relationship to its own clients, and which has accordingly shifted its attention away from the basic business practice of providing a good service for a good price. The recent financial crisis would not have been possible in a culture in which bankers were concerned about making sound loans rather than generating fees for their own profit while packaging and reselling faulty mortgages to other investors to avoid incurring the losses associated with the bad loans their practices made possible. Cultural norms have an impact on how well markets work. So our economic lives depend on the functioning of two spheres, the market and the government, both of which depend on the cultural sphere for the quality of their performances.

Benedict's encyclical goes on to argue that we need to place more weight on the cultural sphere, and that one way of doing so would be to create space for commercial entities that embody virtues of gratuitousness and mutuality that are necessary for the economy as a whole to function more humanely. Such "hybrid" firms demonstrate how a transformation of culture is not inimical to the notion of profit.

Further, it is worth noting how the emphasis on the role of culture fits in with a teleological understanding of the economy. Culture simply is where we pursue our ideas about what constitutes human flourishing. Culture is what forms our ability (or lack thereof) to see our lives as integrated wholes. This is the sphere where Church teachings could have a real impact. The concrete economic concerns of the Church for development (nutrition, health care, education, etc.) end up looking much like the list of concerns economists would generate. But these issues have different meanings depending on the cultural setting. For example, a campaign to eliminate illiteracy is likely not the same as the campaign to teach people to read in order to facilitate their project of truth seeking. A program designed to feed the homeless will not work the same way as a program designed to befriend the homeless while at supper. Culture is what potentially gives these goals a thicker meaning.

Culture, of course, is not an institution. Culture cannot be moved in one direction or another by policy prescriptions. Discussion of the cultural sphere and its impact on economic life is thus different from discussion of the other two spheres. Most economic discourse is really aimed at policy prescriptions about what the government should or should not do. It is thus aimed at a decision maker with some sort of power. In order to help the policymaker craft good policies, the economist describes the behavior of individuals, and especially the way that behavior is coordinated and channeled by market forces. Economic discourse is ultimately a language of control.[15] Policymakers cannot control culture, so they ignore it. But cultural changes can have a big impact. It is here that Pope Benedict's proposal to reconceive human relationships can bear much fruit.

Chapter 5

Reciprocity in Economic Life

> Today we can say that economic life must be understood as a multi-layered phenomenon: in every one of these layers, to varying degrees and in ways specifically suited to each, the aspect of fraternal reciprocity must be present.
>
> —Benedict XVI, *Caritas in veritate*, 38

> Reciprocity [is] the heart of what it is to be a human being.
>
> —Benedict XVI, *Caritas in veritate*, 57

One of the most stimulating proposals Pope Benedict makes in *Caritas in veritate* is to acknowledge and encourage reciprocity in economic life. In this he provides both a challenge to how economic life is lived and an implicit critique of scientific economic analysis. As Luigino Bruni and Stefano Zamagni have put it, reciprocity is a daily economic occurrence that is simply overlooked in the mainstream economic paradigm.[1]

On the one hand, economics examines exchanges, explicit contracts between two parties in which there is a specification of the things to be exchanged (typically goods or services moving in one direction and a specified monetary payment in the other) and concerning which both parties recognize that they are entering into a legally enforceable agreement to execute the terms of the contract. On the other hand, economics recognizes a second sort of transaction: a gift, where one person transfers something of value to the other, with no transfer in return. But economics largely ignores reciprocity, which is something of a mixture of exchange and gift. In reciprocity, one person gratuitously provides something to another—for example, holding the door for another whose hands are full or helping to fix a neighbor's broken appliance—and yet there is a general expectation that the recipient of the assistance will return the favor someday, whether to the same person or to someone else. Reciprocity engages us with others. The authors in this chapter provide alternative but mutually supportive approaches to the notion of reciprocity in the thought of Benedict XVI.

RECIPROCITY AND FRATERNITY

STEFANO ZAMAGNI

Pope Benedict speaks extensively of reciprocity in *Caritas in veritate*. But what is the principle of reciprocity? The simplest explanation is to compare the principle of reciprocity with the principle of exchange of equivalent values. The latter principle states that whatever A does or gives to B, with whom A freely chose to start a relationship of exchange, must be counterbalanced by B doing or giving something of equal value to A. This "something," in a market economy, is the price.

This principle of the exchange of equivalents has two important features. First, establishing the market price logically precedes the transfer of value from A to B. If A wants to sell his house to B, they must above all reach an agreement on the price, and only afterward can they go on to transfer the right to the property. Second, the transfer from B to A is not freely determined; on the contrary, it depends on the transfer from A to B. In fact if B refused to fulfil the agreement, he would be compelled to do so by law. This means that in the exchange of equivalent values, there is freedom beforehand, since the parties to the agreement are not forced to negotiate, but there is no freedom after the agreement is struck.

In reciprocity, by contrast, neither of these two features exists. A acts freely to help B in some way based on the expectation that B will do the same, eventually, for him or, even better, for a third person, C. In reciprocity there is no previous agreement on price (i.e., how B will reciprocate), nor is B obliged to repay A or anyone else. Person A simply forms an expectation, and if that expectation is disappointed, A puts an end to (or changes) the relationship with B. This is why reciprocity is a fragile interpersonal relationship: the person who initiates the relationship always runs the risk of running into an opportunist who only takes and never gives.

The principles of reciprocity and exchange of equivalents also differ in two other ways. First, the value of what B will give to (or do for) A or C need not be equivalent to what A gives B. Reciprocity, in fact, is based on proportionality, not equivalence, as Aristotle understood perfectly: each person gives according to his or her real possibilities. On the other hand, while the primary motive of the exchange of equivalent values is the pursuit of a (legitimate) interest, reciprocity always starts as a free gift: A approaches B with the attitude of someone who wants to make a gift, not to make a deal.

Pope Benedict's stress on reciprocity makes clear that *Caritas in veritate* is a call to overcome the now-outdated dichotomy between the economic and the social spheres. Modernity has left us as a legacy the idea that access to the economy requires setting profit as the main goal and being moved by self-interest, which is the same as saying that one cannot be a true entrepreneur if one does not pursue profit maximization. This absurd idea derives from the theoretical error that confuses the market economy, a genus, with one of its particular species, namely capitalism. This error, in turn, has led us to erroneously identify the economy as the place where wealth (or income) is produced and the social sphere as the place where wealth is distributed and solidarity is found.

Pope Benedict's encyclical, on the contrary, reminds us that it is possible to do business even while pursuing socially useful goals and acting for prosocial reasons. This is one of the possible tangible ways to bridge the dangerous gap between the economic and the social sphere. While it is true that an economy that eliminates the social dimension is not morally acceptable, it is equally true that a social sphere consisting solely of redistribution, completely ignoring the production of wealth, would not be sustainable in the long run. One can only distribute what has been produced.

We must be especially thankful to the pontiff for challenging the erroneous commonplace that economic activity is too serious and difficult an activity to allow it to be influenced by the four cardinal principles of the social teaching of the Church: the centrality of the human person, solidarity, subsidiarity, and the common good. From this same mistaken commonplace comes the false practical conclusion that the principles of the social teaching only apply to works of a social nature, since the task of leading the economy must be left to the efficiency experts. This encyclical does a great service in correcting this serious cultural and political error.

Contrary to what people commonly think, the basic principle for telling what is and is not a business enterprise is not efficiency, for the simple reason that efficiency is a means and not an end. It is obvious that one must be efficient in order to attain in the best possible way the end that one has freely chosen. However, the choice of ends has nothing to do with efficiency in itself. Only after the end has been chosen can the entrepreneur act efficiently. Efficiency as an end in itself becomes the ideology of efficiency, which today is one of the most frequent causes of the destruction of wealth, as the current economic-financial crisis sadly confirms.

A second great service that *Caritas in veritate* offers us is the endorsement of a species of market, typical of the traditional "civil economy" school, according to which one can live the experience of human sociality inside a regular economic life, and not outside or beside it, as the false dichotomous model of economy and society suggests. This point of view is an alternative both to the liberationist idea of the market as the locus of exploitation of the weak by the strong and to the libertarian idea of the market as the place where all the problems of society can be solved.

Civil economy is an alternative to the economic tradition descending from Adam Smith, which tends to see the market and the night watchman state as the only institutions that democracy and freedom really need. Catholic social teaching instead reminds us that a good society depends on markets and freedom, but also that many disadvantaged people have unmet needs that must not be ignored, nor left to the private sphere of voluntary service and philanthropy. Catholic social thought does not side with those who fight against the markets and who see economic action as in perennial conflict with the good life. Rather, the Catholic approach proposes a multifaceted humanism where the market is neither resisted nor controlled but allowed to flourish once circumscribed by an appropriate juridical framework.

Of all the elements essential for such a resolution of our economic problems today, the one most frequently overlooked is fraternity, a word enshrined also in the motto of the French Revolution but later dropped by the postrevolutionary order and eventually eliminated from the political and economic lexicon. But it was the much earlier Franciscan school of thought that gave the word *fraternity* the meaning it kept over time, for fraternity is what completes that which the solidarity principle leaves undone. For as solidarity is the principle of social organization that enables unequals to become equals, fraternity is the principle that allows equals to be different. Fraternity allows people who are equal in dignity and in their fundamental values to make different life plans, or to express their charisms in different ways. The nineteenth and, even more, the twentieth century were characterized by great cultural and political battles in the name of solidarity, and this was certainly positive; just think of the history of labor unions or the struggle for civil rights. But the good society cannot be satisfied with solidarity alone, because a society based only on solidarity and not on fraternity would be a society that everyone would try to escape. While a fraternal society is based in solidarity, the contrary is not necessarily true.

Without both solidarity and fraternity we will not find a credible solution to the great trade-off between efficiency and equity. A society without an active fraternity is not capable of generating a future; a society where one can only give to get or else give out of duty is not capable of progress. This is why neither liberal individualism (where nearly everything is exchange), nor state-centred collectivism (where nearly everything is prescribed) is a safe path out of the ideological swamps in which our modern societies are mired.

RECIPROCITY, TRUST, AND SOCIAL CAPITAL

DANIEL K. FINN

In *Caritas in veritate*, Pope Benedict recommends humanizing economic life by introducing into it "the logic of gift." As he says, "in commercial relationships the principle of gratuitousness and the logic of gift as an expression of fraternity can and must find their place within normal economic activity" (*CV*, 36). And the means for accomplishing this, the pope argues, is reciprocity, which is "the heart of what it is to be a human being" (*CV*, 57).

But in spite of such universal sentiments to apply reciprocity throughout the economy, Pope Benedict spends most of his time and attention in the encyclical on small economic organizations, alternatively referred to as small "hybrid forms of commercial behavior" or "enterprises in pursuit of different institutional ends" or "commercial entities based on mutualist principles and pursuing social ends" (*CV*, 38). These firms earn a profit but spend a sizeable portion of that profit in service to others beyond the firm. Largely ignored in this analysis is the immensely larger group of ordinary firms where the vast majority of people work. Broadening the scope of reciprocity to include this larger group can provide two advantages: improving the accuracy of the discipline of economics in its mission to describe what goes on in economic life and assisting those involved in ordinary for-profit businesses to envision and embody a deeper form of daily economic interaction.

It is helpful that Benedict starts with this small group of small hybrid firms to prove the existence, characteristics, vitality, and value of reciprocity, but the great challenge is to extend it: both descriptively (acknowledging and celebrating its partial embodiment within many other firms) and prescriptively (encouraging more workers, managers, and owners of ordinary firms to engage in it).

Thus, consider two examples of reciprocity in "ordinary" market situations. First, there is the entrepreneur who receives a rush order and makes a request to work the next three Saturdays to his foreman (who will have to persuade his crew to do the same) to complete the order on time. There may be no contractual obligation for the foreman to put in the overtime, but it would not be at all unlikely that in a spirit of cooperation the foreman agrees to oversee the process. The foreman willingly "does the favor" for his boss, but he also has the general expectation that his boss will return the favor someday. When the foreman later asks a favor, the boss will typically grant it. And of course the same logic of reciprocity will exist between the foreman and the workers he asks to work overtime. The informality and ongoing character of trust make all this possible and in fact make for a richer and more humane workplace than would be the case if both management and labor simply "work to contract."

But this sort of reciprocity occurs also quite frequently between the businesses, particularly when there is a personal relationship among the agents of a business, most often between the owners of two small firms who do business with each other, but possible even among managers in two larger firms who deal with each other on an ongoing basis in the market. In an exchange, a price is set before the exchange occurs, but in many exchanges between firms there are unique circumstances and a particular price is worked out at the beginning of each agreement. It is not infrequent among small businesses that one firm gives another firm a break because of extenuating circumstances and then expects a similar favor in return at some future time. These events can look to the scientific observer like two separate, legally enforceable contracts, but they form a sequential interaction that includes at least a dose of reciprocity.

Of course, this very tendency of "mainstream" economics—to impose on the actors it studies its predetermined interpretation of human motivation and meaning—raises issues in the philosophy of social science that we cannot go into here.[2] But the point is that the inclusion of reciprocity within economic analysis could improve both the descriptive adequacy of economics and its capacity to understand and predict economic behavior, even by its own current standards and methods. In this sense, the pope's insight into reciprocity can improve the economist's understanding of social capital, which can best be understood as a stock or pool of trust in an organization or society. Trust between persons is then understood as a flow that contributes to building up social capital. Reciprocity is that set of actions and expectations that produces and sustains trust.

But separate from the economic analysis of these activities, the notion of reciprocity can also articulate how a Christian or Catholic view of economic life can have an impact on economic life itself. If we understand reciprocity in the broader sense as occurring within and among much larger and more diverse kinds of firms, then employers, managers, and owners of all firms might more self-consciously take notice of the dimension of gratuitousness already existent in their economic relationships and to take steps to deepen them. Reciprocity could, then, be understood to characterize—at one end of the spectrum—some economic interactions very close to but not identical with contractual exchange, and—at the other end—economic interactions very close to but not identical pure gifts. (And of course there is a long history within the discipline of anthropology of attending to the phenomenon of reciprocity in gift giving.)[3]

Unlike in hybrid firms, profit here might be sought with little or no intention to send profits anywhere but to stockholders, and yet profit could be understood as being earned in the midst of relationships of reciprocity, recognizing that other firms are also potentially involved in a process of reciprocity. These sorts of interactions have been modeled within game theory under conditions of repeated rounds of interaction, with actors developing "reputations" that others consider in bargaining with them, but this analysis still employs (a refined version of) the self-interest paradigm and does not understand relationships deeply. Rooting such interactions in the notion of reciprocity, with the concomitant dimension of gratuitousness and attention to relationship, would stress their inherently moral dimensions more authentically.

An additional concern in any effort to broaden the scope of reciprocity is a caution about the use of overly personalized descriptions of what reciprocity entails. In an effort to identify the more personal characteristics of reciprocity, *Caritas in veritate* speaks of fraternity, a notion that would seem to work better in Europe than in the United States. While it is true that the notion of *fraternité* as articulated in the French Revolution embodies important values that Catholic social thought would want incorporated in economic life, there are significant difficulties with the English equivalent—certainly in the United States and perhaps elsewhere in the English-speaking world.

One of those difficulties is that for many in the United States, *fraternity* refers to an organization of young and stereotypically immature males on a college campus. The other, more significant problem arises from the perspective of gender. The existence of the word *sorority* implies that *fraternity* refers to males only. While this sort of exclusive language made social sense at the time of the French Revolution, following the developments of the women's movement in recent decades, such an androcentric term is not likely to be sustainable for the future. It is possible that the untranslated *fraternité* could work, but that would be a solution for scholars only and would not likely be functional for others in the United States.

The pope seems to presume that solidarity of itself does not include fraternity (*CV*, 13). But if we side with Wittgenstein and take the view that the meaning of a word is its use, this conviction would seem to be a matter of definition, not something in the nature of things. The apparent meaning of *solidarity* in the document (basically a morally valuable but impersonal relationship characterized by justice) excludes the more personal and vivid concern for others that Pope John Paul II intended when he used the word *solidarity*. In *Centesimus annus*, John Paul argued that previous popes had used other terms for what *solidarity* conveyed: friendship (Leo XIII), social charity (Pius XI), and a civilization of love (Paul VI) (*CA*, 11). But even if it is ultimately necessary to limit the notion of solidarity to justice without the personal dimension embodied in *fraternité*, a word other than *fraternity* will most likely be needed in the United States.

THE LOGIC OF GIFT AND THE WORLD OF BUSINESS

MICHAEL J. NAUGHTON

Pope Benedict's proposal to understand the nature and purpose of business under the umbrella of "logic of gift" immediately confronts a serious problem within business today: the resistance to recognizing the gifted character of business. Mainstream business theory and practice has unfortunately failed to see capital as a form property with a social and spiritual nature and labor as a form of work with moral and vocational meaning.

Josef Pieper argued that the key to the moral and spiritual crisis of modern society is the refusal to accept a gift. He pointed to "the strange propensity toward hardship that is engraved into the face of our contemporaries as a distinct expectation of suffering."[4] He asked whether this propensity toward work, toward career, toward achievement, toward technology is perhaps the deepest reason for the "refusal to accept a gift, no matter where it comes from."[5] Have we lost the ability to receive gifts? Are we unable to think with a logic of gift? Have we deluded ourselves into thinking that everything is earned or achieved?[6]

Pope Benedict engages this modern problem by pointing out how this dynamic between receiving and giving must be informed by charity. He defines charity as "love received and given" (*CV*, 6). The phrase is the beginning of what we mean by a "logic of gift." This logic of receiving and giving is like the inhaling and exhaling of life. It begins to describe the dynamic relationship between the contemplative and active life within the person, which informs the nature of relationships that are first and foremost expressed in family and faith communities, but also in work communities. There are three particular claims that this dynamic and complex operation of receiving and giving brings with it, and each claim informs how we can understand business through a logic of gift.

The first claim is that at the heart of how we develop as persons is the dynamism of love, which entails both receiving and giving. In the first sentence of the encyclical, Benedict explains that this charity "is the principal driving force behind the authentic development of every person and of all humanity" (*CV*, 6). These two fundamental dimensions of our lives—of giving and receiving, of action and contemplation, of work and rest—are not simply two isolated periods of time in human life. As Karl Rahner explains, they are "moments in a person's self-realization which exist only in their relation with one another and are the primary constituents of human existence itself."[7]

The second claim is that the receiving dimension of this charity has a certain primacy. The structure of this love "expresses the primacy of acceptance over action, over one's achievement."[8] David Schindler expresses this well: "When we first experience our being as created, as being gifted life, this *receiving* enables us to see our *doing* and *having* as ways of *giving* which they are meant to be."[9] This is why Benedict, as Cardinal Ratzinger, argued that the person "comes in the profoundest sense to himself not through what he does but through what he accepts," not through what he achieves but what he receives.[10]

The third claim, which builds upon the prior two, is that if this deep receptivity fails to animate organizational life—that place where we are so often asked to give of our time, our talents, and ourselves—we will find ourselves in a disordered relationship in every exchange. This is why Benedict explains that "the great challenge before us . . . is to demonstrate, in thinking and behavior . . . that in commercial relationships the principle of gratuitousness and the logic of gift as an expression of fraternity can and must find their place within normal economic activity" (*CV*, 36). This logic of gift begins to describe a business as a community of persons that stands in contrast to a society of individuals expressed in terms of shareholder or even stakeholder models (*CV*, 39). If business is to be a place where people can integrally develop as persons, business must make room and provide space for a logic of gift that orients people to deeper levels of communion, solidarity, and fraternity.[11]

Chapter 6

Business

> Today's international economic scene, marked by grave deviations and failures, requires a profoundly new way of understanding business enterprise. Old models are disappearing, but promising new ones are taking shape on the horizon.
>
> —Benedict XVI, *Caritas in veritate*, 40

Not only does Pope Benedict provide *Caritas in veritate* with deep theological roots, but the branches of the tree extend into the practical world of business, where Benedict acknowledges the difficulties presented by a focus on profit alone and calls for a rethinking of the foundational purposes and culture of enterprise.

Critical to such efforts are new understandings of leadership as bearing a spiritual dimension and of business itself as worthy of theological reflection. Only with an interdisciplinary approach—certainly possible at any Catholic university with both a business school and theology department—will a proper reconception of business be available to business leaders facing global pressures today.

LEADERSHIP ETHICS AND *CARITAS IN VERITATE*

LUK BOUCKAERT

One of the most important recent developments in the ethics of business is spiritual-based leadership, many of whose practices are inspired by a Western interpretation of Eastern philosophies: Buddhism, Taoism,

Japanese Budophilosophy, Yoga, and mindfulness. Most of them are now practiced and developed in a Western style as tools for a happy and successful life. *Caritas in veritate,* with its focus on love as a universal and cocreative force within people (see the introduction), its plea for a holistic and personalist idea of development (chapter 2), and its awareness of the role of spiritual knowledge in social theory and practice (this chapter), adds a Christian anthropological dimension to the entrepreneurial interest in spiritual-based leadership.

Defining integral development, Pope Benedict refers to the human soul and its aspirations as the ground beneath spiritual-based leadership:

> The question of development is closely bound up with our understanding of the human soul, in so far as we often reduce the self to the psyche and confuse the soul's health with emotional well-being. These over-simplifications stem from a profound failure to understand the spiritual life, and they obscure the fact that the development of individuals and peoples depends partly on the resolution of problems of a spiritual nature. . . . The human being develops when he grows in the spirit, when his soul comes to know itself and the truths that God has implanted deep within, when he enters into dialogue with himself and his Creator. (*CV,* 76)

There are two important practical consequences to draw from this insight. First, if we want to relate economic growth to integral human development, it has to entail spiritual growth. But how can a manager or business leader know whether the economic indicators of a firm's growth foster or hinder spiritual growth? The answer implied in the pope's statement is a very simple but challenging one: the leader can take himself or herself as a barometer. Does the path taken by economic growth in the company make the leader a more human and spiritual being, living in harmony with his or her deeper self? If not, the company's growth strategy has to be questioned. Spiritual growth as such cannot be measured by external indicators (even though some conditions that can stimulate spiritual growth can be measured). It can only be recognized by internal reflection. Hence the importance of an inner-driven and reflective commitment of the leader.

But internal reflection is not a sufficient condition to foster spiritual-based leadership. A second conclusion to draw from the pope's statement is that spiritually driven leaders of tomorrow must be trained in seeing, analyzing, and discussing the spiritual dimension of economic and social problems. Therefore they need not only a personal commitment but also an appropriate conceptual framework and an engaging language, enabling them to analyze the spiritual nature of social problems and to communicate with believers and nonbelievers about these problems. In this context, it is important not to restrict the idea of spirituality to an exclusively Christian or traditionally religious terminology. Theological debates about identity claims would be a distraction; what is needed are inclusive theories and practices enabling people to discover their own spiritual potential and to develop a spiritual art of leadership. The pope clearly envisages a form of wisdom integrating spiritual awareness in the field of knowledge:

> Knowing is not simply a material act, since the object that is known always conceals something beyond the empirical datum.... It requires new eyes and a new heart, capable of rising above a materialistic vision of human events, capable of glimpsing in development the "beyond" that technology cannot give. By following this path, it is possible to pursue the integral human development that takes its direction from the driving force of charity in truth. (*CV*, 77)

How might this attitude of contemplation in knowledge and decision making be cultivated into a profane theory and practice of leadership? How might the art of spiritual leadership be introduced? One way to proceed is to build on three "spiritual competencies": the art of questioning, the art of listening, and the art of decision making. These arts cannot be learned by applying formalized models of decision making, but only by the teaching of a good and wise master, the effort of personal reflection, the study of good and bad examples, and the experience of success and failure.

First, the art of questioning aims at deconstructing conventional wisdom in order to open the mind for something beyond the empirical datum (*CV*, 77). In the Socratic method, the art of questioning is central because no one can reach a deeper level of understanding without standing outside the fixed knowledge of the past and opening one's mind for the unknown. This method of learning by questioning also appears in the teachings of Jesus and the Buddha and in the stories of the Talmud.

The Socratic dialogue is a method to make people aware of the invisible source of their knowledge and action. We cannot reach that deeper level of understanding without giving up the dominance of pragmatic and rational knowledge. The return for this loss of pragmatic and rational control of things is an access to the intuitive and spiritual layers of consciousness, which are the humus from which entrepreneurial creativity sprouts. If leaders want to uncover this source of creativity in people and organizations, a necessary step is to organize within a company a space of deep questioning.[1] Deep questions concern the identity and the core values of a company. What kind of organization do we want to be? What are the unsolved questions in our business? What are the contradictions between our personal and our organizational values? Are our values defined in terms of past identity or controlling ethical codes, or are they seen as levers to explore the unknown and to "disclose new worlds"?

Second is the art of listening, which is complementary to the art of questioning. In *Theory U*, Otto Scharmer nicely distinguishes four basic types of listening.[2] He relates each type of listening to a concrete linguistic expression:

1. *Yes, I know that already*. By this expression, listening is considered as a form of downloading, as a way of reconfirming habitual judgments; listening is a déjà vu experience.
2. *Oh, look at that*. By this statement we pay attention to facts and to novel or disconfirming data. This form of listening is practiced in good science.
3. *Oh yes, I know how you feel*. This is an expression of empathic listening. Instead of looking at things as an outsider staring at the objective world, we move into the subjective and inner world of persons. This form of listening connects us directly to other living beings and activates the "intelligence of the heart."

4. *I can't express what I experience in words.* My whole being has slowed down. I feel more quiet and present and more my real self. I am connected to something larger than myself. Scharmer calls this level of listening "generative listening" or listening from the emerging field of the future. While empathic listening is embedded in our relation to a human person or a living being, generative listening is connecting us with something that is unknown but experienced as a presence larger than ourselves.

In Scharmer's terminology, generative listening is the experience of "presencing" the emerging future. From a Christian perspective, we may relate this experience to the presence of the Divine Spirit at work in human history. Many great leaders (e.g., Gandhi or Mandela) refer to this manifestation of the Spirit or the Divine as the inner compass of their leadership. Peter and Kirstin Pruzan's book, *Leading with Wisdom,* provides a concrete insight into the way some business leaders today conceptualize and practice the spiritual art of listening, by providing the results of fifty in-depth interviews with important business leaders all over the world.[3]

The third spiritual competence is the art of decision making. The most frequently used method of decision making in economics is the rational cost-benefit analysis. Its weakness is that it erroneously presupposes that all relevant costs and benefits are both known and quantifiable. But unpredictability and creativity can never be fully captured empirically. We need other methods in addition to anticipate what is not yet there and to evaluate what cannot be measured.

In his *Spiritual Exercises,* Ignatius of Loyola distinguishes two ways of arriving at a sound choice. The first way he calls the discernment of spirits. This approach asks the individual to examine his deeper moods when considering the range of options open to him and to imagine which of these options would most likely lead to an enlargement of spirit (*dilatatio*) or inner comfort (*consolatio*). This approach principally emphasizes what happens with and to the individual during a process of choice. The second way relies on the *ratio,* which systematically lists the advantages and disadvantages of each option so as to weigh up what, in the long term, would be the most favorable solution. This latter type of consideration can be found in rational choice theory. Ignatius regarded the spiritual and rational approaches as complementary, but the spiritual as being the most decisive in making choices of great importance, where we commit ourselves to a relatively unknown future and are dependent on our deeper, inner compass.

Spiritual-based decision making in business deserves far more exploration but it is clear that Pope Benedict's *Caritas in veritate* pushes us all in this direction and calls attention to the resources for conceptualizing an effective and spiritually fulfilling leadership within the Catholic tradition.

THE BUSINESS ENTERPRISE

MICHAEL J. NAUGHTON

In *Caritas in veritate,* Pope Benedict claims that what is required in today's economy is "a profoundly new way of understanding the business enterprise" (*CV,* 40). He explains that this rethinking "requires a deeper critical evaluation of the category of relation. This is a task that cannot be undertaken by the social sciences alone, insofar as the contribution of disciplines such as metaphysics and theology is needed if man's transcendent dignity is to be properly understood" (*CV,* 53).

This theological and interdisciplinary rethinking is not Benedict's alone.[4] In the United States, several business leaders and academics have made a similar call. Robert Greenleaf, back in the 1970s, also noted the important role of theology in engaging this "category of relation" to institutions. He coined the phrase "theology of institutions," where he argued, "we have much *science* of institutions, but little *theology* of institutions."[5] In 1990, Michael Novak called for a "theology of the corporation," recognizing the dearth of theological reflection on the growing influence of the corporation.[6] More recently, Gary Hamel, a leading business scholar in the United States, wrote in the *Harvard Business Review* that an important challenge for management is to "reconstruct management's philosophical foundations." This "will require hunting for new principles in fields as diverse as anthropology, biology, design, political science, urban planning and theology."[7]

What is needed in the United States and in the Church is an engaged interdisciplinary and theological exploration that brings to bear upon the nature and purpose of business (and of organizations more generally) a deeper notion of relationships and community. Within an increasingly technological, consumerist, and careerist culture, we are confronting the limits of a bankrupt vision of the person and institutions. What Benedict, Greenleaf, Hamel, Novak, and others are telling us is that we need to embed our understanding of business and organizational life in a larger transcendent reality that has the capacity and the resources to order our interests, profits, and contracts to a good that develops us in relationship to others. We and our organizations need integral human development.

This interdisciplinary and theological synthesis can and must be expressed in a publicly accessible way with people who do not share this theological ground. But if we sever our theological roots in order to make ourselves relevant to a larger pluralistic public, we will find ourselves like cut flowers, which wither and atrophy. Our aim is to be like a tree with deep roots that has the ability to weather the difficulties that confront us.[8]

But where can such a theological and interdisciplinary conversation take place?[9] It would seem that such an understanding of the firm could be developed within Catholic universities, in particular in collaboration between their theology departments and business schools. With over 200 Catholic universities in the United States alone, most of whom have some kind of business program, one would expect that such places would afford the richest of resources for such a conversation. Unfortunately, for the most part, neither business schools nor theology departments have pursued this possibility.

Many Catholic business schools get nervous with theological and, in particular, ecclesial language. They tend to ignore or suppress it. Porth, McCall, and DiAngelo surveyed Catholic business schools and found that most had mission statements, and many had references to ethics, but very few connected mission or ethics to the Catholic character of the university.[10] When ethics was mentioned, it was a secular understanding of ethics and typically tended to be utilitarian.

Theologians, for their part, have mostly ignored business questions, expecting their colleagues in philosophy to engage the field of business ethics. While there is a strong interest in Catholic social thought among theologians, there is a tendency for that interest to focus on either political questions or macroeconomic issues. Theology as a discipline has tended to see politics, not business, as the instrument of economic justice, and has avoided the need to educate leaders within business to change their own institutions.[11]

The theological insight of Benedict's "logic of gift" should serve as a basis to understand business as a community of persons.[12] Rather than being an imposition from outside, it provides as an important source for understanding the nature and purpose of business. This understanding of business stands in contrast to the dominant view of business in the United States, which views the firm as a society of individuals expressed in terms of what is commonly known as the shareholder or stakeholder model. The promise of *Caritas in veritate* is that both firms and those who work within them can have a different future: richer, more productive, and more fulfilling.

Chapter 7

Development

> Authentic human development concerns the whole of the person in every single dimension. Without the perspective of eternal life, human progress in this world is denied breathing-space. Enclosed within history, it runs the risk of being reduced to the mere accumulation of wealth; humanity thus loses the courage to be at the service of higher goods, at the service of the great and disinterested initiatives called forth by universal charity.
>
> —Benedict XVI, *Caritas in veritate,* 11

> The truth of development consists in its completeness: if it does not involve the whole man and every man, it is not true development.
>
> —Benedict XVI, *Caritas in veritate,* 18

Pope Benedict dedicated *Caritas in veritate* in a special way to his predecessor Paul VI, and his often-overlooked 1967 encyclical *Populorum progressio.* The theme for both documents is development, focusing on Paul VI's notion of integral human development—in application of social teaching to the economic problem of the development of poor nations, but also describing the authentic development of each human person. Neither individuals nor nations can flourish without attention to the deeper needs and destiny of humanity.

Such concerns raise both empirical and normative questions. Once we agree on a paradigm for defining development in a wider sense of well-being or human flourishing (whether for poor or wealthy nations), a first question asks what well-being and flourishing are and whether they can be measured to check on the effectiveness of efforts to achieve this thicker understanding of development. This also raises questions of strategies behind international economic assistance (foreign aid) and the relative importance of individual effort and institutional change in those strategies. *Caritas in veritate* does not provide detailed answers here, but it does indicate some directions for movement that can provide real help to development professionals and ordinary citizens. The authors in this chapter, coming from policy science and economics, provide a diversity of perspectives and questions, helping to enrich the notion of economic development implicit in Pope Benedict's encyclical.

HOW MUCH OF TRUE DEVELOPMENT CAN BE MEASURED?

MARY JO BANE

Economists and policymakers have by tradition narrowly limited their goals for economic development, but this is no necessity. An interesting example of ways of thinking about social goals that are not simply material goals is the report by the Commission on the Measurement of Economic Performance and Social Progress, established by French president Nicolas Sarkozy and chaired by the economists Joseph Stiglitz and Amartya Sen. The commission aimed

> . . . to identify the limits of GDP as an indicator of economic performance and social progress, including the problems with its measurement, to consider what additional information might be required for the production of more relevant indicators of social progress; to assess the feasibility of alternative measurement tools, and to discuss how to present the statistical information in an appropriate way.[1]

The commission's report has three main sections, one of which examines indicators of "quality of life," based on the recognition that economic well-being, even if better measured than it currently is, is only one dimension of a good or satisfying life. The report is primarily empirical rather than normative. It does not attempt to define the good life but instead explores aspects of well-being that are important to a range of constituencies and which also have been studied empirically. Beyond material living standards, these aspects include health, education, personal activities including work, political voice and governance, social connections and relationships, environment, and insecurity. The commission also explores subjective well-being, the answers of survey respondents to questions about their happiness, their satisfaction with their lives, and their positive and negative feelings at specific times.

Pope Benedict begins his discussion of "human development in our time" with a description of Pope Paul VI's "articulated vision of development" in the encyclical *Populorum progressio*:

> He understood the term to indicate the goal of rescuing peoples, first and foremost, from hunger, deprivation, endemic diseases and illiteracy. From the economic point of view, this meant their active participation, on equal terms, in the international economic progress; from the social point of view, it meant their evolution into educated societies marked by solidarity; from the political point of view, it meant the consolidation of democratic regimes capable of ensuring freedom and peace. (*CV*, 21)

This formulation is not all that different from the conceptual framework used by Stiglitz and Sen. The basic convergence would seem to invite a potentially constructive dialogue about human development, with the potential for generating attention to noneconomic but widely shared and measurable aspects of satisfactory lives. Catholic social teaching could contribute a richer concept of a well-lived life than is currently captured by self-perceived happiness and life satisfaction. To Paul VI's formulation, Benedict adds respect for life and religious freedom as important aspects of development. One can also imagine, even in the standard empirically based social science approach, adding the notion of whether people feel that their life has meaning or is directed to a goal larger than themselves. Exploration of these concepts could broaden the dialogue, without being perceived as sectarian.

Looking more broadly in his encyclical, we see that Benedict includes openness to gift and giving in his notion of integral human development. This is a novel addition to the dialogue on quality of life but would not be inconsistent with some commonly cited empirical findings. Social science research has established the importance of relationships and social capital in people's assessment of their well-being. There is also interesting research on the importance of religion, especially religion practiced in community. Positive feelings have been found to be associated with giving. We can also observe widespread engagement in community service and other volunteer activities; we often hear the phrase "giving back" voiced as an aspiration for their lives by many.

The ideas surrounding gifts and giving are a potentially rich contribution to public dialogue. They capture a widely shared sense that life on this earth is a precious gift, given to all of humanity, and the foundation of our shared membership in the human family. For people of faith, God is the source of the gift, but an appreciation of the fact that much of what we have has been neither earned nor deserved by us individuals is part of many secular worldviews as well. Gratitude for what has been given, whoever or whatever the giver, is a widely shared, attractive feeling that can generate both deep personal satisfaction and an openness to sharing with others. The dialogue on quality of life is likely to become important in policy discussions and it could benefit from the insights of Catholic social thought in struggling to define and observe it.

EXPANDING THE ECONOMIC PARADIGM OF DEVELOPMENT

MARY L. HIRSCHFELD

If we attend to Pope Benedict's hopes for economic life in *Caritas in veritate*, it is clear that the central contrast is between authentic (or integral) human development and the sort of development that proceeds "by merely technical progress and relationships of utility" (*CV*, 9). The concrete description of development he offers (*CV*, 21) contains a set of goals that are in the main the same ones development economists and policymakers would point to: the eradication of hunger, deprivation, endemic disease, and illiteracy, equal access to international economic processes, and the building of democratic regimes capable of ensuring freedom and peace.

Benedict adds a fourth goal, evolution of societies marked by solidarity, that might not make an economist's list of desired goals, but which would arguably fit in with notions of development such as the one advocated by Amartya Sen or by the Stiglitz-Sen commission just described by Mary Jo Bane.

The encyclical's list of obstacles to development is also quite similar to the list economists might develop: excessive income inequality, corruption and illegality, a failure to respect the human rights of workers, mismanagement of international aid funds, and cultural models and social norms of behavior that hinder development.

So the pope's concrete articulation of the goals of development and the problems that hinder its achievement seem to be not materially different from the ones economists would invoke. Yet the encyclical distinguishes between integral human development and other, presumably inauthentic or nonintegral, concepts of development. So what is lacking in the more secular understanding of development?

According to the encyclical, the inadequate concept of development involves a dominance of the pursuit of private interest and the logic of power resulting in social fragmentation (*CV*, 5); it is interested in "merely technical progress and relationships of utility" (*CV*, 9) and is mostly "technological" (*CV*, 23); and it can be reduced to "mere accumulation of wealth" (*CV*, 11). The encyclical implies that there is an important difference between mainstream economics today and the Church's understanding of economic activity as embedded in a human life oriented toward particular ends.

Economic theory assumes that individuals maximize their expected utility (or happiness). This entails some argument that individuals efficiently translate their time, income, and other resources into happiness, with due accounting for uncertainty and the costliness of acquiring knowledge. This assumption is made partly because it allows for the employment of mathematical models of human behavior, but also partly because it resists any judgment by the economist on the individual's personal conception of what constitutes happiness. By avoiding the question of whether individuals successfully convert their economic resources and time into genuine human flourishing, economists are forced to focus instead on how best to accumulate the means by which we pursue happiness—most notably income (or economic output, which is the same thing).

However, this bracketing of the question of what constitutes human flourishing is problematic on several fronts, even using nontheological criteria. It makes the odd assumption that whereas we can progress in knowledge about how to convert our resources (time, skills, etc.) into goods and services, there is no need to worry about whether we are also progressing in our knowledge about how to convert those goods and services into human flourishing. There are many reasons to challenge that assumption. Empirical studies suggest that the correlation between income and subjective reports of happiness are not nearly as strong as economic theory would imply. First, the logical argument used to justify the assumption that firms maximize profits (that firms who fail to maximize profits will be driven out of business) cannot be applied to households (since households that fail to maximize utility are not driven out of business). Second, the new and thriving field of behavioral economics is confirming what psychologists have long told us about the limits of human reason.

Without the assumption that increases in income result in an improvement in human flourishing, standard models of economic development become inadequate. Policies that increase income might or might not be compatible with an increase in human flourishing. To take a domestic example, an important plank in Reaganomics was to adjust tax rates in order to encourage greater work effort. But such policy proposals failed to acknowledge the assumption that the increase in output is worth the decrease in leisure, something required for those policies to be deemed successful. Economists are well aware that a measure of resource endowments is an inadequate measure of a nation's well-being because what matters is not the amount of resources, but rather the efficiency with which they are used. But they rarely notice the parallel argument that it is a mistake to assume income is a measure of well-being without asking about how well it is transformed into genuine human flourishing.

While some economists are aware of these sorts of issues, even they typically fail to see just how pervasive and important they are. In any case, it is salutary for the Church to remind us that genuine human development requires attention not just to the economic means of pursuing human flourishing but also to the adequacy of our conception of human flourishing. It may be more difficult to measure, but if there is no increase in wisdom to match the increase in technological prowess, the technological prowess is as apt to be as harmful as it is to be helpful.

Caritas in veritate also argues that integral human development should be understood in light of our ultimate end, which is transcendent, and that human flourishing is not adequately understood against a purely horizontal horizon:

> Without the perspective of eternal life, human progress in this world is denied breathing-space. Enclosed within history, it runs the risk of being reduced to the mere accumulation of wealth; humanity thus loses the courage to be at the service of higher goods, at the service of the great and disinterested initiatives called forth by universal charity. (*CV*, 11)

If death is absolute, security takes on an excessive, even idolatrous weight, which makes it more difficult for people to sacrifice or risk sacrifice for either higher goals of their own or the good of the neighbor. In addition, the loss of a transcendent horizon can shunt our transcendent yearnings into pursuit of finite goods, with the result that our desires can never truly be satiated. In such a world, scarcity is inescapable, and with scarcity comes the logic of opportunity cost and trade-off.[2] So, for example, the decision for altruism is assumed to come at the expense of pursuing one's own well-being.[3] The combination of excessive concern for security and insatiable yearnings places an accent on material well-being that distorts human life. Indeed, this would be yet another reason to strongly doubt that untutored human choices are ordered to genuine human flourishing.

The pope goes on to argue that integral human development is primarily a vocation involving a free assumption of responsibility in solidarity on the part of everyone (*CV*, 11). We do not create meaning; we affirm it by responding to the call to love God and our neighbors, and by working out our particular role in God's plan. As the pope writes, "to regard development as a vocation is to recognize, on the one hand, that it derives from a transcendent call, and on the other hand that it is incapable, on its own, of supplying its ultimate meaning" (*CV*, 16). The economist's accent on subjective happiness simply repeats the modern notion that humans create meaning rather than receive it. The Christian account instead focuses on the sort of wisdom that grasps the true aims of our lives, which in turn should serve to order our economic strivings. It is a journey of discovery, which, as Augustine tells us, informs us of the nature of our destiny only after we have embarked.[4]

The argument about the importance of ordering our economic strivings to some sort of end, and the further argument that our end is properly transcendent, serve as genuine critiques of economic thought and have important implications for concrete policy debates. It is an approach that does not so much seek to replace economic argument as to strengthen it by reminding economists of the subordinate role of economic striving in a genuinely human life. However, a lot of deep thought about policy issues will be needed to incorporate the genuine insights of economists into this larger theological or philosophical framing. Benedict's encyclical calls us to such work in the coming years.

INTERNATIONAL AID: CHARITY IS INSUFFICIENT

KATHERINE MARSHALL

Pope Benedict's encyclical, *Caritas in veritate*, argues that we must travel "the path of development with all our heart and all our intelligence, that is to say, with the ardor of charity and the wisdom of truth" (*CV*, 8). It highlights the "dangers of utopian and ideological visions" and states quite baldly that "the idea of a world without development indicates a lack of trust in man and in God" (*CV*, 14). It calls for a "profound and far-sighted revision of the current model of development, so as to correct its dysfunctions and deviations" (*CV*, 32). Its provocative suggestion of unfinished intellectual business after the unraveling of the communist world deserves exploration.

Thus, we can and should probe what that "new model" truly looks like and how it differs from the current "best-practice" thinking within development circles, as well as from the more grueling on-the-ground day-to-day realities of development work.

There are many areas of congruence that suggest good potential areas for dialogue and collaboration: a far greater appreciation today of what is entailed in "holistic" development, less linear thinking on development aid as a panacea, more focus on community development and "ownership" in various forms, and increasing focus on governance.

Nonetheless, the encyclical underscores the significance of active and unresolved debates around the rationale for development assistance in U.S. policy. Some of these tensions are probably inevitable, as there will never be a single reason for any dimension of international or other relationships. However, the overlapping arguments, often obscured in rhetoric, that characterize much discourse on U.S. international development policies do constitute a significant problem both in communication and in execution. At a minimum, clarity and honesty of thinking are needed, along with some ordering of priorities.

Is charity, that is, compassion and magnanimity, the primary rationale for U.S. assistance (for example, in responding to Haiti's earthquake, Pakistan's floods, or Africa's doldrums)? Or is the underlying rationale more akin to a focus on self-interest? Is there and should there be an appetite for, or at least an acceptance of, a social justice approach that is linked in some fashion to a notion of a "right to development"? How do we acknowledge and appreciate the security dimensions of assistance and the role played by both security arguments and military or security assistance? And, embedded in the rationale for microcredit and even more in "bottom of the pyramid" policies, there are arguments for economic self-interest—benefits that are to flow back to donors from broader economic growth.

The best approach—and one with strong support in Catholic social teaching—would be a robust commitment to development assistance, akin to a Marshall Plan, with the United States taking up a leadership mantle for the rights-based approach as opposed to the compassion or self-interest rationales.

But even this initial orientation leaves a host of practical questions to address. What does this imply about the level and modalities of financial assistance and its organization? What is the best balance between public responsibilities and private development? How does the significant but now flagging interest in microcredit and support for small business fit into such a commitment? What about public and private roles in education and health? What is a sensible approach to dialogue about these important but complex issues?

Caritas in veritate is clear in its admonition that richer nations (the United States is plainly at the fore) have an unambiguous responsibility to provide increased development assistance: "More economically developed nations should do all they can to allocate larger portions of their gross domestic product to development aid, thus respecting the obligations that the international community has undertaken in this regard" (*CV*, 60). Where does that leave the United States on the embarrassing challenge (embarrassing because it is honored in the breach) of each wealthy nation dedicating seven-tenths of one percent of GDP for development, in particular to support the officially endorsed Millennium Development Goals?

More specifically, the arguments of the encyclical point to the need for a rethinking of charity (in its various dimensions) in contemporary society. This is timely, since we face today not only great problems but a new capacity for ending poverty that we simply did not possess in the past.

We need a discussion of philanthropy and its role, which in turn raises questions about the purposes of wealth. Is wealth solely a means or should it have some recognition as an end? What is the responsibility of the wealthy? What is the appropriate role of contemporary charity, individual and "mass" (via the Internet, for example)? The evolving balance between the social responsibility of companies and broader social entrepreneurship and catalytic roles of philanthropy presents many practical challenges.

Pope Benedict presents powerful arguments both for putting high priority on development and for a linked, holistic approach to sustainable development, one that links aid and trade. It makes a strong case for a more coherent U.S. foreign assistance strategy—balancing country ownership with overall, global strategies and standards, community focus with strategic good sense. The encyclical's arguments for cultural intelligence and for good governance would be welcome enrichments of development debates.

DEVELOPMENT AND INSTITUTIONAL FAILURES

STEFANO ZAMAGNI

The encyclical *Caritas in veritate* deals powerfully with the link between integral human development and institutional design. In our time the market—and the culture of contract on which the market is based—has grown progressively more important in daily life. There are those on the right politically who believe that the global market will and should re-create social obligation and rebuild human relationships, and they want everything in our social, political, and cultural life to be directed to the efficiency of mechanisms and the effectiveness of procedures. The "good news" of competition and globalization, a sort of gospel for some, seems to have become the dominant ideology, a sort of "single thought."

However, Christians believe that we need a new human dimension to all this integration of national economies through the market. A good model of development must generate not only efficiency but also well-being, considering the whole human being—in all dimensions—and all human beings, bearing in mind the right of each individual to realize his or her potential and aspirations. Thus *Caritas in veritate* emphasizes the totality of human development without rejecting the market, private enterprise, profit, or finance.

The encyclical holds that everyone should help make the rules and build the institutions, to select the aims and decide the priorities, by which the economy is governed. And if in the teachings of the Church there is criticism of the dominant model of development, this is not because the Church underestimates the enormous benefits such development has brought to humankind but because such development is too often exploited to create inequalities rather than to enhance solidarity, to increase what is superfluous rather than to redistribute necessities, to impose the dominance of one particular model of development rather than to acknowledge the resources of different approaches.

A hasty reading of *Caritas in veritate* might lead one to believe that the criterion used to shape institutions ought to be efficiency. And to some it might seem true that when in a given moment in history certain rules are followed instead of others, it is because these rules have proven to be more efficient than the alternatives. But there are two main reasons why both of these impressions are false. First, the concept of efficiency, as it is used in economics, is not a primary concept, as it comes from Jeremy Bentham's utilitarian principle, which is neither an economic principle nor the only possible standard for gauging efficiency. Therefore efficiency cannot be said to be a neutral or objective assessment criterion—a criterion to be used to make the market work at its best. Let us recall that the market economy existed long before utilitarian philosophy entered economics.

Second, in calculating efficiency, the social externalities (both positive or negative) of the economic activity are not taken into account. Consider the frequent situations where efficiency is opposed to fairness or freedom in its positive sense. If in order to achieve a more efficient result positive freedom must be sacrificed, what then guarantees the sustainability of the market institution over time? In the short term, economists can abstract from this concern, but the market cannot exist in the long run without freedom. On the other hand, economic development is the result of factors that do not belong solely to the economic sphere. Emile Durkheim warned that the values of society are not mere means at the disposal of economic calculation, given that society can always oblige or compel its members to act so as to neutralize the injunctions originated by that calculation.

Benedict XVI calls on economists to reconsider critically the renowned thesis that the market is self-legitimizing and therefore not subject to moral constraints. Those maintaining this thesis start with the fact that "both parties in an economic transaction benefit from it, provided that the transaction is bilaterally voluntary and informed."[5] As a consequence, when two (or more) parties honestly and voluntarily originate an economic transaction, they also agree to any consequences. This is the ethical justification of consequentialism in economics. The concept of consent based on freedom of choice is well explained by Richard Posner: "I personally believe that he who buys a lottery ticket and loses, agrees to the loss if there was no fraud or coercion."[6]

From such a perspective, choosing freely means giving one's consent, and agreement provides legitimization. As is argued by Fabienne Peter, the market does not need to ask for a certificate of ethical legitimacy, because it is capable of legitimizing itself.[7] This is not the case for the state which, on the contrary, in order to be able to use coercion needs the approval of the electorate, for only from them can the state be legitimized.

What is wrong with this reasoning? Basically, it is almost never true that freedom of choice entails real consent. It would be so if the one choosing had taken part in the creation of the choice menu—but this is almost never the case in real life. The parent voluntarily offering, under no obligation of any kind, to sell one of his organs to alleviate the poverty of his family certainly does not agree to the consequences of his act. Free choice of an option has the power to legitimize only if the set of alternatives is somehow part of the subject's choice problem. If this set is given, this prerequisite is by no means fulfilled.

Consent is central to the tradition of social contract theory starting with Thomas Hobbes. The idea is that if in the past I have signed a contract with you to do something I now no longer want you to do, your answer could be, "But you agreed to do it at the time; now you have to abide by the terms of the contract." In Thomas Hobbes's world, consent generates obligation. Among those who embrace the social contract theory, John Rawls was best able to show that in order for consent to produce obligation, the constraints under which the parties to the contract take their decisions must be shared by everyone. Only if it can be proved that the parties to the contract agreed (or intended to agree) to the rules of the game they are in can it be legitimately claimed that the agreement reached through consent implies obligation.

Of course, it is evident that in our market economies this condition is never fulfilled in practice. Indeed, this faulty view of freedom of choice is defined by the absence of coercion by others. It has to do with the possibility of choice, that is to say, with the existence of a domain or space within which the subject can exercise his sovereignty. But this still says nothing about the ability to choose, in other words, the real exercise of the choice. Having a large number of possible choices is not enough if you do not know how to choose or if you do not have the resources to translate the means into the capability of promoting your own goals. This is the great lesson taught by Benedict XVI when he reminds us that the use of freedom is essential to its definition. Someone who is "free" to put into practice his action plan, but who does not possess the capacity to do so, cannot really be said to agree to the consequences of his actions. Therefore, if the market is not capable of finding within itself the reasons upon which to construct its justification, it requires an ethical foundation outside the market.

In an authentic understanding of development, the encyclical *Caritas in veritate* moves freely, like an amphibian, among the various arenas of study dealing with human action in all its multiple forms. In this, the pope proposes a resolution of the dispute between two competing schools of thought that, in order to shed light upon important dynamics of our society, end up either dissolving subjectivity into community (i.e., neo-Marxism or neo-structuralism) or glorifying subjectivity and thereby reducing social issues to a mere set of individual preferences (i.e., liberal individualism). The pope proposes an approach that is both morally and empirically superior, celebrating human subjectivity but always within a network of communal ties and obligations, with both person and community formed by humanity's ultimate destiny.

Chapter 8

Polarization

> Hence charity and truth confront us with an altogether new and creative challenge, one that is certainly vast and complex. It is about broadening the scope of reason and making it capable of knowing and directing these powerful new forces, animating them within the perspective of that "civilization of love" whose seed God has planted in every people, in every culture.
>
> —Benedict XVI, *Caritas in veritate*, 33

> Because it is a gift received by everyone, charity in truth is a force that builds community, it brings all people together without imposing barriers or limits.
>
> —Benedict XVI, *Caritas in veritate*, 34

Few features of contemporary life are as debilitating as polarization, the acerbic opposition and at times the mutual demonization that occur across lines dividing people of different fundamental convictions. Pope Benedict's encyclical *Caritas in veritate* is founded on the presumption that careful thinking and conversation can assist the Church and each of its members to become clearer in recognizing the truth of the gospel and more receptive to its message, even if it challenges personal or cultural presumptions. Polarization is a sign of deep resistance to fundamental questioning and is a rejection of the *caritas* that Benedict teaches should accompany even the most deeply held of truths.

To begin, it is helpful to consider the polarization that accompanied the appearance of the encyclical this volume reflects on and to ask whether *Caritas in veritate* itself may inadvertently exhibit some of the forces behind polarization in its dual insistence on the importance of dialogue between world religions and on its own proclamation of the truth as understood by the Catholic Church. Nonetheless, the encyclical does indeed propose resources that hold out hope to reduce polarization in both public and private life. The authors in this chapter come from divergent backgrounds and provide differing analyses. In this very diversity, they provide a mutually reinforcing sense that, in spite of challenges, even within Catholic social thought itself, Benedict's hope is indeed well founded.

THE PROBLEM OF PUBLIC POLARIZATION

JOHN L. ALLEN

The first wave of Catholic commentary on Pope Benedict's *Caritas in veritate* was striking, but not because the verdict was mixed: American Catholics, notoriously, would have a hard time agreeing on what day of the week it is, so one hardly expects a univocal reaction to a papal encyclical. One was instead struck by how preexisting ideological filters seemed to drive competing perceptions. At the time, I playfully wrote that partisan reactions on the American Catholic Left and Right could be tagged the "Khrushchev letter" and the "Blue Meanies" strategies, respectively.

The Catholic Left often seemed to approach the encyclical like the Kennedy administration approached communications from Soviet Premier Nikita Khrushchev during the Cuban Missile Crisis—responding to what they liked and just disregarding the rest. Hence liberal commentators hailed what Benedict had to say about labor unions, redistribution of wealth, and a planetary form of governance, but largely glossed over his treatment of "life issues," including abortion, birth control, gay marriage, and population control. Reading some progressive Catholic commentary, it was as if sections 15, 28, 74, and 75 of *Caritas in veritate,* devoted to bioethics and the defense of human life, simply were not there. That is all the more remarkable given the point Archbishop Giampaolo Crepaldi made in presenting the encyclical to the press: Benedict's integration of anthropology and social ethics—his integration of *Humanae vitae* and *Populorum progressio*—is arguably the single most distinctive element of *Caritas in veritate.*

On the right, another game was afoot—finding a cabal of Blue Meanies in the Vatican to blame for the sections of *Caritas in veritate* that many conservatives found troubling. The clearest example came from George Weigel, who distinguished between "gold passages" in the encyclical, which he believes come from the pope himself, and "red passages," which Weigel ascribes to a "social justice crowd" concentrated in the Pontifical Council for Justice and Peace, which he believes is still smarting from the blow their anticapitalist agenda took with *Centesimus annus*.[1] The point of that reading, of course, is to suggest that only the gold passages actually merit what canon law describes as "religious submission of mind."

In their book *Attacco a Ratzinger*, Italian journalists Andrea Tornielli and Paolo Rodari include backlash against *Caritas in veritate* in the United States from what they described as "theo-cons," citing Weigel and Michael Novak, as part of the broader "attack on Ratzinger." As Tornielli and Rodari put it, "It's a sign that criticisms of Benedict XVI come from across the board, not just from one part of the contemporary intelligentsia, meaning the progressives."[2]

To be fair, both of these readings responded to something real. The Left was correct that some elements of *Caritas in veritate* clash with strict laissez-faire dogma—though anyone who knows either Catholic social theory or Benedict's own biography should hardly find that surprising. (As a footnote, the Holy Father's great-uncle, Georg Ratzinger, was a populist campaigner against the Bavarian equivalent of robber baron capitalism in the nineteenth century, advocating for laws against child labor and in favor of a minimum wage.) The Right was likewise correct that there are internal tensions and unresolved questions in *Caritas in veritate*, and reductionist readings that would turn Benedict XVI into the chaplain of the antiglobalization movement are simply silly. Pushed too far, however, both these readings seem terribly partial, evocative of what Ned Flanders of *The Simpsons* once described as "strainin' to do some explainin'."

This clash of Khrushchev letter and Blue Meanies hermeneutics offers a concrete instance of a deeper fact of life about American Catholicism, which is conventionally referred to as "polarization," meaning the clash between an ideologically defined left and right. In truth, American

Catholicism may be less polarized than it is "tribalized," since the sociological situation is generally defined by clustering into a variety of ecclesiastical tribes: *Communio* Catholics, peace-and-justice Catholics, liturgical traditionalists, Voice of the Faithful, and on and on. In principle, such diversity is a blessing, but it becomes dysfunctional when these tribes begin seeing one another as the enemy. For some time, the most glaring example of dysfunction in American Catholic life has been precisely the rupture that *Caritas in veritate* rejects: the split between the pro-life wing of the Church and its peace-and-justice contingent.

Of course, the idea that defending unborn life and defending the poor go together is hardly revolutionary at the level of principle. It has been repeated so often in official Catholic literature that there are probably T-shirts someplace emblazoned with that mantra. Statements of principle, however, fail to account for the gap between what we say and what we do. Both at the grass roots and among the chattering classes, pro-life and peace-and-justice Catholics in America generally move in separate circles. They read their own journals and blogs, attend their own meetings, and have their own heroes. Pro-lifers tend to be drawn into the Republican orbit, while peace-and-justice types are more comfortable with the Democrats. As a result, they travel down separate paths, have separate conversations, and invest their time and treasure in distinct, and sometimes even opposing, efforts.

Recent years have seen some noble attempts to put Humpty-Dumpty back together again. When the U.S. bishops produced their most recent version of "Faithful Citizenship," a statement on faith and politics, they styled it as a joint project of their pro-life and peace-and-justice committees. At the time, it seemed a tribute to a unified Catholic vision, though some of that synthesis seemed to unravel under the pressures of the 2008 presidential campaign. A second example is the annual Social Ministry Gathering in Washington, again under the aegis of the U.S. bishops, which has become a laboratory for a consistent life ethic. Yet such efforts remain rare and to date have not had a noticeably transformative effect on American Catholic life.

Tribalism, to be sure, is hardly just a Catholic problem. It is fueled by deep patterns in American social life that work against any effort to transcend divisions. Journalist Bill Bishop has coined a term for the broad tendency of Americans during the past thirty years to retreat into like-minded tribes, both physically and virtually; he calls it "the Big Sort." It describes the reality that more and more, Americans are choosing to live, work, socialize, and even worship only with people who already share their values and worldview. The innovation is not that we are divided, because Americans have always been fractious, but that increasingly Americans who think differently about important matters are becoming strangers to one another—and it is much easier to demonize a stranger than a friend. Bishop says the results of the Big Sort are obvious: "Balkanized communities whose inhabitants find other Americans to be culturally incomprehensible; a growing intolerance for political differences that has made national consensus impossible; and politics so polarized that Congress is stymied and elections are no longer just contests over policies, but bitter choices over ways of life."[3]

Implicitly, Benedict's encyclical raises the hard question of whether American Catholics are fated to replicate these secular patterns within the Church—which, to date, we seem to have accomplished with breathtaking fidelity. Can the Church in America develop a way of "breathing with both lungs," bringing its pro-life and peace-and-justice energies into greater alignment? Or must we settle for a "Big Sort Catholicism"? Can we evangelize secular politics in America, or are we destined to be evangelized by them?

RESOURCES FOR REDUCING POLARIZATION IN GOVERNMENT

MARY JO BANE

In the United States, the biggest challenge for those concerned with bringing the perspective of Catholic social teaching into public life today is to say something reasonably concrete about policy without being or being perceived as inappropriately embroiled in right-versus-left or republican-versus-democratic politics. American politics has become increasingly polarized in recent decades, and increasingly reflective of the divide between conservative churchgoers and the less religious. This polarization certainly inhibits the ability of government to get anything done and may threaten the political stability of the country. In thinking about Catholic social teachings and American politics, the goal must be, at the very least, to do no harm by not contributing to the polarization, and at best to help overcome it.

The Catholic bishops in their 1986 pastoral letter *Economic Justice for All* tried to meet the challenge of teaching specifically about economic and social issues while avoiding politics by clearly distinguishing their discussion of the Christian moral vision of economic life, based on scripture and ethical norms, from their discussion of specific economic issues and policies:

> Our judgments and recommendations on specific economic issues, therefore, do not carry the same moral authority as our statements of universal moral principles and formal church teaching; the former are related to circumstances which can change or which can be interpreted differently by people of good will.[4]

Their judgments and recommendations were indeed interpreted differently, by people of good (and also, probably, bad) will. The most spirited discussion arose around the roles of markets and government, production and redistribution, and the relationships among them. The bishops did not succeed in being perceived as nonpolitical. Their letter was portrayed as leftist, emphasizing government and redistribution. Its defenders and its critics argued in predictably political terms.

The last encyclical in the social justice tradition before *Caritas in veritate*, John Paul II's *Centesimus annus*, won praise and criticism from both Left and Right. Issued after the fall of the Soviet Union by a fiercely anticommunist pope, the encyclical praised democratic capitalism and free markets, while at the same time recognizing that markets need to be both regulated by government and supplemented by other institutions in order to achieve development of the whole human family. The dialogue continued to focus along predictable political lines, at least in the United States, with the Right emphasizing its sections on markets and the Left emphasizing its sections on their limitations.

Caritas in veritate is generating some of the same sort of predictable, politically divided response, partly because it does seem to include something for everybody to both love and hate. The political Right blogosphere praises its emphasis on life issues and its enthusiasm for markets; the Left praises its concern for the poor and its commitment to justice as well as charity. One could with a little effort derive much of the agenda of the Obama administration (save for its support of abortion and gay rights) from the encyclical. Similarly, much the platform of the Republican Party could also be educed from it by emphasizing different sections.

It is more interesting and more important, though, to ask whether there are themes in the encyclical that lead to different ways of thinking, perhaps ways of thinking that might bridge some of the American political divides in the interests of a more truly humane society. Two of the encyclical's themes are plausibly nonpartisan and potentially divide-bridging, and also have interesting complements in recent social science thinking: the theme of integral human development and that of gratuity and communion.

This is an opportune time to explore these themes because the economics profession, so long predominant in policy discussions, is both changing and being challenged. It is changing from within as a result of "behavioral economics," which recognizes and attempts to explore the fact that people do not base their actions on economic self-interest alone. It is being challenged from the outside because of its failure to predict, prevent, or agree on remedies for the massive collapse of financial systems and economies in 2008.

Traditional ideas about government are also being challenged, with the public's massive distrust of government reinforced by partisan politics (as well as by the actual failures of government to perform well). At the same time, huge public problems like unemployment, education, and the deficit are not being dealt with. This should, therefore, be a good time to think about new ways of addressing human concerns.

What this means is that the elite policy dialogue in the United States appears to be more open to ways of thinking about two very broad sets of questions.

The first concerns the goals of social institutions and process. If material goods (the production of things measured by GDP) are not all important, how can our policy objectives and our measures capture the other things that matter? Catholic social thought contributes the notion of integral human development; social science is contributing research on happiness, satisfaction, and the measurement of well-being.

The second set of questions asks which institutions and social processes are best suited to achieve these broader goals. The old arguments about markets versus the state are made less relevant both by a broader conception of development and by new research showing that human behavior is not well characterized by a narrow focus on material incentives. Catholic social teaching contributes the concepts of gift and giving, gratuity and communion. New policy thinking and new technology contribute new models of social interaction and new ways of addressing barriers to full human development.

Thus, not only does Pope Benedict call for an integrated approach to many of the most important problems we face, he does so at a time when independent shifts in social science and in social policy discussions hold out some real hope of overcoming the sharp polarization that typifies so much of contemporary debate within both the Church and state today.

HOPE IN POLARIZATION

AMELIA J. UELMEN

As we increasingly move in a virtual world that seems to be more subject to the control of our own choices, we face the danger that the growth of super-specialized interest-based virtual communities fosters a kind of polarization that makes it difficult to communicate across any kind of political, social, cultural, or ideological difference. Part of the problem might be grounded in social and culture architectures that squelch opportunities for constructive encounters with real difference. But the root might also be one of attitude.

What would it take to get people to want to seriously engage the differences that would otherwise make them uncomfortable, and to want to do the serious work of finding ways to communicate across these differences? A Christian model of communion in which individual identities are not "submerged" but are made "transparent to each other" and linked "more closely in their legitimate diversity" (*CV*, 53), in which "true openness does not mean loss of individual identity but profound interpenetration" (*CV*, 54), might be exactly the resource we need to melt the current structures of polarization. It would also provide the opportunity to live in an authentic way the relationships that allow personal identities to mature (*CV*, 53) and to assume together the "joyful task" of "working for the benefit of all" (*CV*, 78).

Chapter 9

Language and the Orientation to Dialogue

Reason always stands in need of being purified by faith.... For its part, religion always needs to be purified by reason in order to show its authentically human face. Any breach in this dialogue comes only at an enormous price to human development.

—Benedict XVI, *Caritas in veritate*, 56

The close relation between faith and reason is fundamental to the Catholic view of the universe: since everything has been created by God, insights of reason into how things work cannot ultimately be at odds with the insights provided by faith and divine revelation. Pope Benedict's intimate interweaving of charity and truth—*Caritas in veritate*—stands as a testimony to the conviction that what we can express in language can serve the ineffable mysteries known only by faith. This means, however, that our use of language should be as careful and our dialogue as effective as we can make them.

One of the great advantages of the Catholic intellectual tradition in engaging secular discussion of public policy today is its traditional appreciation of reason. In the early Church, bishops were often chosen from among the brightest and most educated of Christians—meaning, of course, educated in the best schools of the Greek and Roman world. A number of the Fathers of the Church were, like Ambrose of Milan, adults in successful careers, fully developed intellectually, prior to their conversion to Christianity and their acceptance of leadership roles in the Church. Even those brought up in Christian families showed great respect for philosophy and the insights of the pagan intellects of ancient Greece and Rome.

The system of natural law developed later by Thomas Aquinas argued for the usefulness of human intellect, even when unaided by revelation, in sorting out many moral questions. It was exactly this confidence in reason that led so many popes since Leo XIII to engage debates going on in the secular world around them. They were able to speak a philosophical language accessible to nonbelievers—speaking of rights, subsidiarity, human dignity, and the common good—without having to fear they were undermining the theological foundations beneath these conceptions.

Nonetheless, this great strength of Catholic social thought bears, like all great human strengths, its corresponding liabilities. No application of the Catholic tradition to contemporary policy issues should ignore those shortcomings.

THE NEED FOR ACCESSIBLE LANGUAGE

JOHN A. COLEMAN

As has been amply noted in chapter 2, one of the great strengths of Pope Benedict's *Caritas in veritate* is the deep theological grounding he gives for his approach to economic and political problems.

However, the correlative dilemma to the decided achievement of a grounded theological account for Catholic social teaching—especially in an encyclical that lifts up interdependence, the global quality of social problems demanding concerted global cooperative action—is the lack of a common, theological language to describe the "humanum" (*CV*, 55). After all, *Caritas in veritate* was addressed to "all people of good will." Some greater care seems needed to translate its insights into language that does not depend so heavily on a theological warrant, an important dimension of a vision that can forge the kind of cooperation for human development the pope proposes. The concept of a dialogue of cultures, so conspicuous in *Populorum progressio* (whose fortieth anniversary the pope commemorates in *Caritas in veritate*) is less available in

Benedict's encyclical. It is difficult to find communicative partners for joint action construed so explicitly in Christian theological categories. Fortunately, it is clear that Benedict is not ready to abandon the earlier Catholic emphasis on natural law. Our task is to engage in dialogue in our densely pluralistic world, drawing upon a less theologically weighted account of what constitutes our joint world, vision, and vocation to integral development.

THE AMBIGUITIES OF ACCESSIBLE LANGUAGE

MARY L. HIRSCHFELD

The fundamental idea of *Caritas in veritate* is "that authentic human development concerns the whole of the person in every single dimension" including "the perspective of eternal life" (*CV*, 11). The distinction between authentic human development and more secular notions of human development signals room for a genuinely theological contribution to questions about economic life. But what sort of language is suitable for such a task?

Economic analysis typically seeks to model human behavior with an aim of asking what sort of policy (or lack thereof) best achieves some goal (usually efficiency). The language presumes a binary: either individuals operating through markets make decisions or the state makes decisions. This language is widely accessible, but it is the language of control, because it implicitly addresses some policymaker who seeks to manipulate economic activity toward some desirable outcome, by changing incentives so as to change the choices individuals make.[1]

Caritas in veritate emphasizes the role of culture, but the encyclical is written in the language of policy prescription.[2] And this kind of language might be what lies behind the idea that we need to create a space for new commercial enterprises that embody a wider set of humanistic goals. These new institutions would be the vehicles for carving a set of cultural concerns into the marketplace. Institutions are the proper subjects of policy prescriptions. Pointing to these institutions gives us a way of trying to inject these cultural issues into economic discourse.

However, there are two problems with this. First, the encyclical uses the language of policy prescription to recommend that space be made for these institutions. Presumably it is government that would act to create this space. But the encyclical has already argued that we need to attend to the cultural sphere precisely because institutions work better or worse depending on the cultural environment. Without a prior change in the cultural space, it is not clear how these new institutions are going to embody the cultural changes we want to effect.

Second, the encyclical is a call for us to rethink our ends, but that call is properly addressed not to policymakers, but rather to all of us as individuals who can participate in larger social conversations about the purpose of economic life. The Church's teachings properly belong to the cultural sphere and would be best embodied in a language appropriate to that sphere. The urgency of the document is that we need to recover a stronger sense of grace and reciprocity in our lives in order to provide a foundation for humane markets and a government that supports our pursuit of the common good.

Cultural change requires conversion, and conversion requires rhetorically effective direct address rather than the impersonal "control" language native to policy discourse. In the language of control, the passive voice is often used, and individuals are referred to as objects to be manipulated. Such language makes it unclear just who it is who is supposed to act. Direct address might exhort individual entrepreneurs to creatively seek ways of acting in the marketplace according to principles other than solely profit seeking, and policymakers (and consumers and other firms) to consider ways such enterprises could be encouraged. Instead, the pope urges that space be created within which "economic activity" can be "carried out by subjects who freely choose to act according to principles other than those of pure profit" (*CV*, 37). The subjects who need to do the actual creative work are not addressed at all, and the passive voice addressed (presumably) to policymakers allows us to wonder just who is supposed to do the secondary work of creating space for the primary actors, or what that secondary work actually entails. It is possible to walk away from such language without feeling personally called to do anything at all.

The encyclical does to well point to the importance of attending to the values and meanings our economic processes are supposed to serve.

However, the adoption of the impersonal rhetoric of economic policy undercuts this move by linguistically stranding us in a world where the only meaningful actions are taken by policymakers. The commercial entities in service of humane goals come across as an effort to offer up a novel new policy prescription. The encyclical's aim is higher than that, but it is betrayed by a language that embodies the market-state binary it aims to undercut.

TENSIONS BETWEEN PROCLAMATION AND DIALOGUE

LUK BOUCKAERT

For all its strengths, *Caritas in veritate* exhibits two critical shortcomings, each ultimately rooted in the form of discourse Pope Benedict chose to employ.

First, there is a glaring absence of interreligious or interspiritual dialogue, a vital lever today in any attempt to alter the world around us. Interreligious and interspiritual dialogue is not just a job for theologians or a private undertaking of a few experts. Religious claims about truth are part of today's social questions, and religious practices of generosity and compassion are part of their answers. As the pope says, religion has a public role to play (*CV*, 56). But should not this view lead to an active interreligious and interspiritual forum for civilizing the global economy? The encyclical provides many warnings about cultural relativism, religious syncretism, fundamentalism, and religious indifferentism, but no real effort is made to elucidate the distinction between cultural relativism and intercultural dialogue. Why do we find in the encyclical no references in the footnotes other than to other encyclicals, Catholic councils, or some Fathers of the Church? If we agree with Vatican II that the Spirit of God is also at work in other philosophical and religious traditions, would it not be appropriate to refer to sources within other parts of the spiritual patrimony of the world?

The problem becomes even more difficult when Benedict describes Catholic faith in a way that shows little respect for nonbelievers: "Without God, man neither knows which way to go, nor even understands who he is and . . . a humanism which excludes God is an inhuman humanism" (*CV*, 78). How can we enter into a "fraternal collaboration between believers and non-believers" (*CV*, 57) if we perceive the nonbeliever as an "inhuman humanist" or as someone who does not know which way to go? Of course, we as Christians must be alert to keep alive the uniqueness of our spiritual path, but inclusive dialogue is a better way to realize this than the use of a language excluding the other as an equal partner.

The second great shortcoming of the encyclical is the lack of self-criticism. There is in *Caritas in veritate* a lot of pertinent criticism of neoliberalism, Marxism, fundamentalism, cultural relativism, trendy spirituality, and atheist humanism, among other things. But no self-criticism. There is no reflection on the failures of Christian communities to install a more just, sustainable, and peaceful world; no reflection about the role of Christian communities in the overexploitation of global resources; no reflection on the nonresistance or even the active involvement of Christian communities in the genocide in Rwanda. Of course, self-criticism must not be based on artificial feelings of guilt but on the search for truth. The relation of self-criticism to truth is a fundamental one in a democratic society.

Having noticed these shortcomings, we must next ask about their causes. Two seem to stand out.

First, the encyclical is written mostly in the style of an ex cathedra discourse, a proclamation of truth. Its tone is abstract and logical, unlike the more democratic style of the well-known pastoral letter of the American bishops, *Economic Justice for All.* The American pastoral letter resulted from a collective deliberative process and was based on a more inductive type of analysis rooted in experience. Based in experience, the bishops' letter was read and debated widely. Unfortunately, Benedict's encyclical will likely be read mostly by theologians and other scholars but not by entrepreneurs, social activists, and political leaders. This is a pity because the document has an important message for them.

Second, although Benedict formulates a principle of dialogue—saying that truth is logos, which creates dia-logos and hence communication and communion (*CV*, 4)—this dia-logos is not interpreted as a social dialogue between equals but as a way of disclosing already held truth through reason illuminated by faith. There is a Platonic concept of truth at work here. For Plato, truth is not a process of social dialogue but requires inner dia-logos, which is the privilege of the trained philosopher, who alone has the right insight. Plato rejected all forms of democracy, which he wrongly thought reduced truth to a confrontation of opinions resulting in relativism, chaos, and anarchy.

In *Caritas in veritate*, we find a similar concept of truth: on the one hand, there is the strong rejection of opinions leading to cultural relativism and religious indifferentism; on the other hand, there is the genuine truth, which is the privilege of the Church. This Platonic and aristocratic concept of truth is tempered by a more personalist stance in some parts of the encyclical, which advocates respect for each person as an autonomous source of love and truth. However, it seems clear that the aristocratic idea of truth is the underlying reason why there is a lack of self-criticism and a reluctance to engage in a real interreligious dialogue. Self-criticism presupposes the idea that our own search for truth is always characterized by the Socratic *aporeia* of "not knowing" and by the Christian awareness of human weakness and sinfulness. Benedict's message would have been strengthened had he included less certainty and more epistemological humility.

DIALOGUE IN LIGHT OF THE SIGNS OF THE TIMES

JOHAN VERSTRAETEN

Many fruitful intuitions are articulated in Pope Benedict's *Caritas in veritate*, including rebalancing of the link between love and justice, the plea for gratuity in the economy, and the revaluation of the civil society. Nonetheless, a fundamental question must be asked: whether this encyclical offers a method adequate to the analysis of the global problems the pope himself acknowledges. The answer is negative, due to a fundamental conflict between Pope Benedict's interpretation of Catholic social thought and the basic insights of Vatican II's Pastoral Constitution, *Gaudium et spes*.

The conflict is between the theology of Vatican II, which pays attention to God's liberating presence in the concrete history of humankind, and Pope Benedict's theology based on an image of God as exclusively mediated by the Church. And the Church in this view is a distinct sociolinguistic reality that brings God's love-in-truth to the world via the truth propositions of the *magisterium*. In the Augustinian worldview articulated by Pope Benedict, the "earthly city" is clearly distinguished from the "heavenly city," and it can be humanized only through a purification of its insights and practices by conscientious choices of individual Christians who put the official doctrine into practice.[3]

In the previous section of this chapter, Luk Boukaert has addressed the underlying commitments that have generated this top-down theology. This essay explores the fact that the underlying spirit of *Caritas in veritate* is fundamentally quite different from the basic intuitions of the authors of *Gaudium et spes*.

For a majority of council fathers, the Church is not a "perfect society," not an entity separated from the world, but a community "linked with humankind and its history by the deepest bonds" (*GS*, 1). This conviction is reinforced by the recognition of God's action in the concrete history of humankind, a vision that later became radicalized by liberation theology's recognition that the poor, excluded, and oppressed "others" are the privileged locus of the in-breaking of God in history. According to *Gaudium et spes*, "the joys and the hopes, the griefs and the anxieties of the men of this age, especially those who are poor or in any way afflicted . . . are also the joys and hopes, the griefs and anxieties of the followers of Christ" (*GS*, 1). This awareness of a profound link between Church and world reflects the view of Marie Dominique Chenu and the priest worker movement, according to which "presence in the world is presence with God."[4]

These opening words of *Gaudium et spes* are also an acknowledgment on earth, thus in the world, that God's kingdom is "already present in mystery," in the realization of "human dignity, brotherhood and freedom, and indeed all the good fruits of our nature and enterprise" (*GS*, 39).

Our challenge is how these two quite different theological interpretations of the relation between the Church and the world can be resolved. The solution cannot be an either/or choice, which would be alien to the complexity of the Catholic tradition. The challenge is to value both the theological legacy of *Gaudium et spes*—which has, as a pastoral constitution of an ecumenical council, epistemological priority over papal encyclicals—and to take seriously the genuine concerns of Pope Benedict for the distinctiveness of the Christian contribution to the humanization of the world. And this resolution must occur without resorting to a cheap harmonization that would subvert the hermeneutic tensions.

The path to an adequate resolution begins with the crucial definition of the task of Catholic social thought that appears in *Gaudium et spes*: "scrutinizing the signs of the times and of interpreting them in light of the light of the Gospel" (*GS*, 4).[5]

"Scrutinizing the signs of the times" is not merely a matter of social analysis but also a truly theological task, based on the presupposition that God is at work in this real history of humankind. The scrutinizing requires us "to decipher authentic signs of God's presence and purpose in the happenings, needs and desires in which this people [the people of God] has a par along with other men [and women] of our age" (*GS*, 11). Such a deciphering of authentic signs of God's presence presupposes, as Erik Borgman highlights, that "God's transcendence cannot be discovered in the exaltation and distance with respect to the concrete and laborious life, but precisely in connection with it."[6]

This discovery is a difficult process since it confronts the Church with the real ambivalences of history and the structures of evil that pervert the process of humanization.

Thus, the starting point of Catholic social thought should not be the Church but the world, including an analysis of the signs of wholesomeness and alienation in the world. This theological process necessarily includes social analysis and ethical reflection because judgments about the world cannot be made on the basis of faith propositions alone.[7] Without social and ethical analysis, the faith perspective loses touch with reality or leads to the construction of a world of pious ideas, which would be more an expression of social alienation than a solution to it. Any theological interpretation must not forget to "track the contours of reality; it has to have accuracy, and not simply imagination or appeal."[8]

Unfortunately, *Caritas in veritate* clearly lacks a sufficient valorisation of social, economic, and political analysis, which leads to a vision according to which social transformation is mainly a matter of individual conversion of the heart and not of changing structures.[9] Following Paul Ricoeur, we know that we realize the good life, together with others, in the context of just institutions. These institutions cannot be developed without a thorough and adequate analysis.

At the same time, *Caritas in veritate* teaches that this scrutinizing of the signs of the times must be done in the light of the gospel. This reference to the gospel is not a matter of supplementing the world with additional truths, nor of using the Bible as reservoir of citations that can be used as illustration of moral insights. We are to read the gospel from the context both local or global in which we live, whether "we" are grassroots movements, bishops, the pope, or his advisors. This produces an interplay between historical experience of context and the abundance of meaning generated by the biblical metaphors and stories. In and through a contextual-hermeneutical relation to the biblical text, we are enabled to see the world in a new light and to discover new ways of being and acting.

Such an interpretive relation with the living text of the Bible gives us, in the words of Jon Sobrino, "new eyes for seeing the ultimate truth of things and new energies for exploring unknown and dangerous paths."[10] As Mendoza writes, it enables us to "hear the cries of those who suffer the injustices in a different key within our consciousness" and enables us "to commit ourselves . . . to alternative actions that will not tolerate the myth of the 'way things are.'"[11]

The plea of *Caritas in veritate* for the realization of an economy that includes gratuity can be considered as such an alternative action. But more innovative thinking and practices should be stimulated. This requires not only analysis of what is but also discerning in the present situation the conditions for emergence of a new future.

In sum, *Caritas in veritate* presents us with many significant insights to assist God's people to confront today's evils and move toward a fuller appreciation of what the gospel requires of us. However, its top-down view of theology and the Church eclipses the need to scrutinize the signs of the times in light of the gospel. Until we engage wholeheartedly in this demanding process, other advice—helpful as it may be—on how to move toward integral human development will not bear much fruit.

Chapter 10

Implications

> Man's earthly activity, when inspired and sustained by charity, contributes to the building of the universal *city of God,* which is the goal of the history of the human family. In an increasingly globalized society, the common good and the effort to obtain it cannot fail to assume the dimensions of the whole human family, that is to say, the community of peoples and nations, in such a way as to shape the *earthly city* in unity and peace, rendering it to some degree an anticipation and a prefiguration of the undivided *city of God.*
>
> —Benedict XVI, *Caritas in veritate,* 7

Christian faith will be fulfilled only in a full communion with God that is impossible in this life, and Benedict's *Caritas in veritate* clearly holds out this ultimate vision as our highest end. At the same time, however, the God who created humanity for fulfillment does not reserve all experience of happiness or flourishing for eternity. Ours is a God who with the offer of divine grace holds us his children responsible for embodying in ourselves, our relationships, and our institutions as much a foretaste of authentic, integrated fulfillment as is possible within a situation characterized by finitude, sin, and ignorance. Thus the implications of Catholic social thought for our social, political, and economic life are, as the 1971 Synod of Bishops put it, constitutive of the gospel.

Sorting through the implications of Pope Benedict's encyclical requires careful reflection from a variety of backgrounds and methods. This will require attention to current cultural and technical trends, and the potential for change in business, government, the Church, and daily civil life. The authors in this chapter, coming from different disciplines and life experience, identify differing implications of Benedict's encyclical, but they nonetheless point to an integrated response to the world's problems by Catholic social thought.

NEW INSTITUTIONS AND SOCIAL PROCESSES

MARY JO BANE

The concepts of gifts and giving articulated by Pope Benedict in *Caritas in veritate* may help us to move public dialogue beyond the dichotomy of market and state. The encyclical hints at this in its discussion of the role of civil society and the potential for partnerships across sectors. Unfortunately, however, the encyclical may leave the impression that gift operates only on the margins of the larger economy and state, due to its strong focus on successful social enterprises, hybrid firms, and public-private partnerships. Thinking somewhat more expansively, the notions of gift and giving could generate a wide-ranging dialogue about the full variety of institutions that humanity can construct and use to further genuine development for all.

These institutions include markets and governments, of course, since time has tested and reinforced their usefulness. There is little controversy now about the efficiencies of markets for production and exchange, or about the necessity of a state for performing both regulatory and supplementary functions. Also accepted without much controversy are the important roles played by organizations of civil society, national and international nongovernmental organizations, local community organizations, and so on. But new institutions are emerging from the technological revolution that have the potential to transform the ways people relate to each other, for good or for ill. Networks of all sorts are becoming much more important features of social life, governance, and production, and have the potential to connect people to address problems in truly innovative ways. New forms of collaborative governance are continually emerging and being put into practice.

Catholic social thought may be able to enter this dialogue in ways that emphasize potentially positive contributions and control some of the negatives.

Information technology has dramatically reduced the costs of both communication and coordination. It has also made it much easier and cheaper for people to find each other to share interests and activities. Internet sites like Facebook, with more than half a billion users, make it simple and inexpensive to coordinate everything from political campaigns to terrorism to thousand-person pillow fights. Information technology is transforming the size, scope, and activities of social networks.

Information technology is also making possible new ways of working that are not dependent on institutional structures or hierarchical management. Wikipedia is probably the best-known example of an incredibly useful tool produced through the cooperative voluntary labor of thousands of users. Sites where photos can be shared, like Flickr, have documented and mobilized responses to political repression and to natural disasters like the Indonesian tsunami and the Haiti earthquake. These tools and the myriad creative ways they are being used are transforming the ways people interact and work gets done.

At their best, when they are both constructive and cooperative, these efforts build on various motivations: curiosity, desires for social connection, desires to do good. It is startling how much time and energy people put into simply staying connected and sharing, and also how much energy and how many resources can be mobilized to solve problems. (Clay Shirky, author of *Cognitive Surplus,* estimates that Americans currently spend 200 billion hours a year watching TV. If even 1 percent of that time were devoted to constructive cooperative projects, twenty Wikipedia-scale efforts could emerge every year.)[1] Of course, these new technologies and ways of working can also be subverted by people violating their norms, and they can be used by groups whose purposes are less benign than calling attention to the plight of earthquake victims. But they are clearly here to stay, and the task for the future will be to figure out best how to fashion norms, incentives, and sanctions to take advantage of their vast potential for good while bounding the potential for harm.

According to David Kirkpatrick, the author of *The Facebook Effect*, the creator of Facebook sees the Internet as having the potential for supporting gift economies alongside market economies—patterns of interaction where people give and share with each other in the expectation that others will also give and share. In a way, his vision is similar to *Caritas in veritate*'s vision of gratuity and communion and its endorsement of reciprocity, analyzed in chapter 6 of this volume. Catholic social teaching could help develop and enrich this vision of new human institutions, with a deep understanding both of the potential of humanity to give and to receive thankfully, and of the sinfulness of humanity that will make the construction of such institutions challenging.

Another new development is the emergence of cross-institutional structures for addressing public problems. These include not only contractual relationships between government and both private and not-for-profit organizations, but also genuine collaborations in which all parties share both the shaping of the goals and the delivery of the product or service. These approaches to public problem solving take advantage of both the creativity and the potential for efficiencies in nongovernmental organizations. They are also, at their best, able to mobilize noneconomic motivations of citizens and community members. The charter school movement, for example, has generated many examples of creative and effective partnership.

There is a potential for Catholic social teaching to help shape a dialogue around these developments that is neither partisan nor polarizing, but that instead bridges some of the traditional divides through a focus on new opportunities. The dialogue could begin with the gospel mandates of feeding the hungry, welcoming the stranger, making peace, and so on, and then move to the question of what institutions and processes are available to address the problems: what combination of markets, state action, voluntary associations, networks, and collaborations are most likely to reflect the values we care about and the realities of concrete situations? The dialogue could be enriched both by the insights of Catholic social thought and by the imaginations of all men and women of goodwill to whom the pope's encyclical is addressed.

A BETTER LEGAL DEFINITION OF WHAT IS REASONABLE

AMELIA J. UELMEN

In *Caritas in veritate*, the life of communion at the heart of the Trinity is a lens through which we can see "all individuals and peoples within the one community of the human family" (*CV*, 54). "God desires to incorporate us into this reality of communion as well: 'that they may be one even as we are one'" (John 17:22) (*CV*, 54). Within this vision, one can see how to open oneself and relate to the needs of others without one's own identity being swallowed in the process, because in the life of the Trinity, "true openness does not mean loss of individual identity but profound interpenetration" (*CV*, 54). In a Trinitarian model, openness to others is not a negative encroachment on one's personhood but actually the positive key to self-fulfillment. Freedom consists of the essential capacity to open oneself to the other. It is, at its core, relational.

In contrast to legal theories that emphasize an effort to balance or manage fairly what would otherwise be competing interests and rights, a Trinitarian model posits that a life of communion is the essence of the structure of reality. Acting in a way that acknowledges the other as the living image of God is a true positive good for oneself as well, and more characteristic of an authentically human life. On the flip side, as Pope John Paul II explained in *Centesimus annus*, "When man does not recognize in himself and in others the value and grandeur of the human person, he effectively deprives himself of the possibility of benefiting from his humanity and of entering into that relationship of solidarity and communion with others for which God created him. Indeed, it is through the free gift of self that man truly finds himself" (*CA*, 41).

What difference might this lens make for aspects of legal theory? Take, for example, the case of the Ford Pinto, which could explode on rear impact, even at slow speeds: even though Ford was aware of the risks, because of a cost-benefit analysis, it had determined it would be cheaper to compensate for resulting injuries and death rather than alert the public and recall the Pinto for repair. The jury was outraged and, in addition to $2.5 million in compensatory damages, ordered the company to pay $125 million in punitive damages. The award was later reduced, but the case remains an important symbol.

While there may be some truth to Milton Friedman's famous claim that the social responsibility of corporations is to generate profits,[2] avoidance of tort liability is also an important part of a healthy profit-generating business. Regardless of intricate economic theories, the common law tort system includes a mechanism of accountability to the larger community as measured by community standards. Even when instructed in economic terms, often a jury will reject a cost-benefit framework and follow their deeper moral instincts. As one law professor put it, "No one has suggested that jurors are deeply conflicted over whether the average person ought to take as much care for the average other person as for himself or herself."[3]

Benedict's "critical evaluation of the category of relation" (*CV*, 53) can shed light on the definition of *reasonableness* that may already be at work in community standards regarding product safety. Within the framework or *Caritas in veritate*, placing the integrity and safety of the human person at the center of production would be interpreted not as a concession to clashing interests, nor as an inconvenient but sadly necessary restriction on freedom, but as intrinsic to the deepest purpose of the businesses involved. When the reference for rationality is relationality, it becomes evident that "rational profit maximizers" might be missing out on the greatest richness of all. Further, given the tendency of civil juries to react with horror to some manifestations of the logic of rational profit maximizers, the model might also serve as something of a shortcut to the working definitions of reasonableness that form the standards to which manufacturers will actually be held legally responsible.[4]

PARTICIPATION AS KEY FOR A JUST ECONOMY

JOHAN VERSTRAETEN

Pope Benedict's call for dialogue and reciprocity in economic life means that it is necessary but not sufficient to give "poorer nations an effective voice in shared decision-making" or to let the poor participate in development programs as *Caritas in veritate* suggests (*CV*, 67). They also must be acknowledged as full participants in all decisions that affect their lives. All too often they are excluded from it. Where is, for example, the participation of indigenous people in the decisions about using their land for the extraction of natural gas in the Peruvian Amazon or in the building of transnational highways in Brazil that cut through the cradle of their native communities?

A number of voices have recently addressed this lack of participation, with focus on civil society and community building at the local level.[5] This is a step forward because it implies that the participation of the poor is not merely economic—acknowledged in part by *Caritas in veritate* by referring to the poor as not a burden but a "resource" (*CV*, 35)—but also political, social, and cultural. Indeed, the very meaning of civil society is that people become full participants in the construction of their communities and societies.[6]

This participation is also implied in the principle of subsidiarity, which starts from the presupposition that people are not simply objects of decisions, nor means for the construction of a good society. A society is not constructed but is brought about by living together, generated and realised by people. Consequently, achieving the common good "implies a high degree of participation in decision making" by "active citizens."[7] Participation in Catholic social thought means "a series of activities by means of which the citizen, either as an individual or in association with others, whether directly or through representation, contributes to the cultural, economic, political and social life of the civil community to which he belongs."[8] For Ivereigh, this means more than voting: "it means acting to change the world around you" and includes the creation of "local mechanisms of participation" and freeing people from the isolation that Pope Benedict XVI describes as one of the deepest forms of poverty (*CV*, 53).[9] In this sense participation is also connected with the preferential option for the poor, which is not simply an option for the poor, but an option to be with the poor, who must be trusted as our companions in the discernment of the requirement of justice in society.

It is important to note that the first level of participation and togetherness is civil society. Civil society is not the same as the *bürgerliche Gesellschaft* based on one's interests and on the belief that economic self-interest contributes to the well-being of all (as Adam Smith has suggested). In *Centesimus annus*, Pope John Paul II rightly criticises the fact that "the individual today is often suffocated between two poles represented by the state and the market place. At times it seems as though he exists only as a producer and consumer of goods, or, as an object of state administration" (*CA*, 9). According to Pope Benedict, "the exclusive binary model of market-plus-state is corrosive of society" (*CV*, 39). This is why we need a vibrant civil society, "where people come together voluntarily to act in and around shared interests and values."[10]

This vision is based on the difference between social contract and covenant. "If the basis of political and economic society is the contract, the basis of the civil society is the covenant," writes Jonathan Sachs, who argues that this covenant is "maintained by an internalised sense of identity, kinship, loyalty, obligation, responsibility and reciprocity."[11] Civil society is, in other words, "the bedrock of democracy, the glue that holds society together. It is neither public (state) nor private (economic) but made up of what are often called 'voluntary organisations'—churches, schools, charities, fraternal organisations, residents' associations, ethnic groups, trade union branches, and so on. . . . Civil society is bound together by the power of association—the bonds formed by values and common interests."[12] It is based on the logic of gratuity and gift and "a force that builds community," as Pope Benedict explains. It is the place where people can again discover the value of belonging; it is the sphere where networks of relationships are generated in which people become persons.[13]

The networks and communities of civil society are places where people are trained to be responsible for others and the community. They also function as mediators between the macro- and the microlevels of action. In a world that has become a society of networks, it is not enough to create civil society organisations—we must work above all to create meaningful connections and bonds.[14] Social networks between individuals and organisations can be very effective in responding to immediate needs, if these include the needy in the decision process. This argument for networks and participation in the civil society, however, should not be used as an argument against just institutions (including just international economic institutions), nor as an argument for the downsizing of social security systems (*CV,* 25). As Michael Walzer argues, "there is no community and no common good without social justice. Political societies cannot survive on evocations of citizenly virtue, responsibility, and fellow feeling. This must also be a commitment in practice to the weaker members. This is a commitment that only the state can make in a universalizing way."[15] Even Amartya Sen maintains, despite his bottom-up approach to justice, that "an appropriate choice of institutions has a critically important place in the enterprise of enhancing justice."[16]

Catholic social thought can play a crucial role in proposing an ethical framework for these institutions, both organizations and networks. But this will be impossible without an open dialogue with all stakeholders. The Trinitarian character of the life of God as relational, described in chapter 2, means that our lives, work, and institutions must be judged by these very standards of dialogue and participation.

RECONCEIVING WELFARE POLICIES

STEFANO ZAMAGNI

Pope Benedict has provided a ringing endorsement of the logic of gift, but what does embracing gratuitousness in economic action entail practically? Two pressing issues regarding social welfare systems provide vivid examples of the difference the pope's thinking can make.

The first one concerns how we should construct welfare programs. A welfare system should be based upon universal precepts, but can it be designed without creating dependence? In other words, is it possible to conjugate solidarity and subsidiarity, equity, and reciprocity in a credible and sustainable way? Pope Benedict's answer is yes.

The state has three main duties in creating a welfare system: (1) the definition of a set of social services that is guaranteed to all citizens; (2) the fixing of rules of access for those services and therefore rules for the redistribution (taxation) necessary to fund them; and (3) the establishment of controls on the effective allocation of the services to people.

The tasks of directly producing the services or managing their allocation need not be done by government. Yet in some situations, the government does itself produce these services—where the providers are themselves government employees—and it can be appropriate if the benefits for becoming the producer exceed the costs of doing so. But the danger is that the greater the state's role as manager, the less will be its capacity to regulate, and thus the less its capacity to ensure the objectives of equity and efficiency that are the hallmarks of any sound social security system.

There are basically three models for welfare systems under discussion in both the political and social scientific arenas. The first is the neostatist model, according to which the state, while conserving its monopoly role as purchaser, should give up its monopoly over the production of welfare services. Known as the *welfare mix*, in this approach the government avails itself of civil society organizations for help in allocating services, yet makes the political decisions on its own. The government is the only agent responsible for formulating and programming the interventions. Such a situation helps us understand the difference between the principle of subsidiarity and the principle of surrogacy. The first declares that the state must promote the organization of civil liberties, favoring all those collective forms of action that have public (i.e., general) effects. The second affirms the contrary. The principle of surrogacy means that intermediate bodies of society should do all that the state is incapable of doing or has no interest in doing.

The second model, known as *compassionate conservatism*, counts on philanthropy and volunteer action to meet the needs of those left behind in society, while government intervenes only in very limited situations. While this model values civil society and its organizations, it undermines the pledge of universal assistance. It is the favorite model of liberal-individualist thought that sees third-sector organizations as a minor segment of the private sphere, but one that is essential to the legitimization of the for-profit logic of the market.

Finally, there is the *civil welfare* model endorsed by *Caritas in veritate*. This model recognizes the ability of organizations of the civil society to become active partners in the process of programming interventions and in the consequent adoption of strategic choices. In practice, this means that it is not enough to recognize the juridical subjectivity of these organizations. What is needed, in addition, is that their economic subjectivity be recognized. It is not enough to ensure their autonomy, in the sense of being able to exist without outside controls. What is also required is financial and economic independence: each organization should have the capacity to realize its own programs and to achieve its own objectives without depending, in a constraining way, on either the government or for-profit firms.

Papal encyclicals do not provide a blueprint for public action or institutions, but *Caritas in veritate* does provide general guidelines that favor some policies over others—in order to assist humanity in moving toward a more integral human development.

SHIFTING ATTENTION WITHIN THE CHURCH

MARY JO BANE

Caritas in veritate has implications for the Church itself, or more specifically for the role of different church institutions and members. Of course, there is today a general skepticism that official church pronouncements will have much direct concrete effect on the thinking or behavior of lay Catholics, not only because the church hierarchy has lost much of its moral credibility in the last few years but also because official pronouncements by any group rarely have much concrete effect. Americans as a whole are not very deferential to authority, and many believe that clergy and church officials should stay out of politics and even out of policy.

But it also seems clear that the values and opinions of Americans are subtly but importantly shaped by their churchgoing, particularly by conversations and interactions with members of their congregational and parish communities. Getting Catholic social teachings into the air—through preaching, adult education, retreats, and so on—so that they shape conversations at coffee hours and Sunday school might be a plausible goal for clergy and lay parish leaders. Catholic parishes might also try to lead by example, to behave both creatively and generously to adopt the new ways of bringing people together and to model as much as possible inclusive dialogue across both religious and political lines.

Catholic institutions of higher education also have a potentially important role in enriching thinking about the interactions of Catholic social teaching and public life and in modeling and encouraging dialogue that moves beyond politics and ideology. To do this well, Catholic intellectuals need to understand not only the teachings of the Church but also the ways in which those teachings can be separated from political divisions and instead modeled and incorporated into the lives of Catholic communities. This is the challenge for those of us who care about our church and care about our country.

DEVELOPING RESOURCES FOR BUSINESS AND BUSINESS SCHOOLS

MICHAEL J. NAUGHTON

If the insights of Catholic social thought articulated in *Caritas in veritate* are to lead to a community of persons informed by a logic of gift in the business world, it will not come from business alone, but from a collaboration with the wider culture, in particular the family, church, and education. Catholic universities serve as an important intersection between Church and world and can play an important role in leading this discussion. One concrete step that could be taken to deepen the role of Catholic universities in the process is the development of two documents (with appropriate processes around such documents), perhaps by the Pontifical Council for Justice and Peace, the Congregation for Education, and Catholic universities. The first document might focus on Catholic social principles for business and the second on Catholic social principles for business education. There are three reasons such documents would be especially helpful in our day.

First, the Church is always in need of greater internal collaboration, specifically between Catholic universities worldwide (approximately 1,000 institutions) and the institutional Church. As business becomes a more global phenomenon, and as Catholic universities wrestle with their own mission and identity, a set of guiding principles grounded in the teachings, thought, and practice of the Catholic social tradition could contribute to both the deeper vocation of business and the renewal of the Catholic university. Here the Church can learn from the UN Global Compact (global principles for business) and a related document called "Principles for Responsible Management Education" (PRME).

Second, although the Church can learn from the UN Global Compact, PRME, and scholars of business ethics and corporate social responsibility, the Catholic social tradition reveals the tensions and contradictions within these approaches, exemplified by the difference between a view of business as a society of individuals and business as a community of persons, as described in chapter 7. Pope Benedict makes clear in *Caritas in veritate* that business ethics severed from a theological anthropology "risks becoming subservient to existing economic and financial systems rather than correcting their dysfunctional aspects" (*CV*, 45). It is important for Catholic universities to articulate their own tradition within their own classrooms; otherwise, the tradition will fail to unfold in a robust manner and contribute to the wider culture.

Third, although the principles of Catholic social thought are essential to understanding social life deeply, the principles tend to be so abstract that many businesspeople are at a loss as to how to put them into practice in business organizations. Consequently, many business executives—as well as administrators and faculty in Catholic universities—consider such principles of little assistance in day-to-day business—or in the curriculum, research, and life of the university. This disjunction between principle and practice is illustrated by a comment from a Catholic health care chief executive on the Church's social tradition. Reflecting upon the principle of the common good, he remarked that it had never helped him to make a decision. The social principles supply us with a sense of that for which we yearn, but their behavioral specificity is thin.[17]

The Church needs to do a better job in helping to translate these principles into the location people find themselves. Documents like those proposed here could articulate Catholic social principles informed by Benedict's logic of gift and community of persons in a way that could help businesspeople and Catholic universities recognize and embody the distinctive elements of the tradition.

IMPROVING BUSINESS EDUCATION

MATTHEW J. SLAUGHTER

Pope Benedict's encyclical calls, explicitly and implicitly, for many changes in "business as usual"—and in this call he is not alone. In the wake of the world financial crisis and the Great Recession, many commentators have assigned much blame to business leaders—and to the business schools from which many of these leaders earned their degrees in years past. As professor and associate dean at one of America's highest-ranked business schools, I take such calls seriously.

Are universities and business schools guilty of malign neglect: turning saints into sinners? No. Business schools are not doing a disservice when they teach a curriculum of finance, economics, accounting, and related disciplines at the heart of global business. Indeed, these building blocks of commerce need to be taught so that future business leaders can better understand the dynamic marketplaces in which they will operate.

Are universities and business schools guilty of benign neglect in not teaching business leaders to think broadly enough about the stakeholders touched by their firms? For at least some schools, the answer is yes. True business leadership, like true leadership in other domains, requires the courage to ask questions and to articulate narratives about goals that are firmly rooted in values. The historical record now shows that before and during the current financial crisis, too few executives and directors in many global financial firms had the courage to ask the most basic of questions, such as, "How do we really know the value of these activities?" or "What happens if that trend line you are assuming will always go up instead goes down?"

At the Tuck School of Business, I have recently overseen the addition to our core curriculum of the requirement that each student complete at least one course on ethics and social responsibility. This requirement exposes students to at least one aspect of the broader social and cultural environments in which today's global businesses operate, with a goal of providing students with facts and frameworks for considering the ethical issues their positions will likely encounter. Such a required course aims to demonstrate in practice and in principle the highest standards to which all business students should aspire.

That said, no such course can be a panacea that will rid the world of business malfeasance. In recent years the average age of the entering MBA classes at Tuck is about twenty-eight. Our students are young adults at the last stage of their formal education, and each already has a personal moral and religious framework that is unlikely to be fundamentally reconfigured with one nine-week course. What guidance might *Caritas in veritate* provide us for understanding responsibility for teaching future business leaders?

Pope Benedict offers insight on how enlightened business enterprises might pursue strategies beyond simply profit maximization:

> Alongside profit-oriented private enterprise and the various types of public enterprise, there must be room for commercial entities based on mutualist principles and pursuing social ends to take root and express themselves. It is from their reciprocal encounter in the marketplace that one may expect hybrid forms of commercial behavior to emerge, and hence an attentiveness to ways of civilizing the economy. Charity in truth, in this case, requires that shape and structure be given to those types of economic initiative which, without rejecting profit, aim at a higher goal than the mere logic of the exchange of equivalents, of profit as an end in itself. (*CV*, 38)

What exactly might these hybrid enterprises look like, and how might business educators examine and teach their merits? Pope Benedict later argues they will likely have features of both the for-profit and not-for-profit structures:

> It is in response to the needs and the dignity of the worker, as well as the needs of society, that there exist various types of business enterprise, over and above the simple distinction between "private" and "public." Each of them requires and expresses a specific business capacity. In order to construct an economy that will soon be in a position to serve the national and global common good,

> it is appropriate to take account of this broader significance of business activity . . . It favors cross-fertilization between different types of business activity, with shifting of competences from the non-profit world to the profit world and vice versa. (*CV*, 41)

How will these organizations be structured and organized? That remains to be seen, but the hope for their flourishing is clearly articulated:

> This is not merely a matter of a third sector, but of a broad new composite reality embracing the private and public spheres, one which does not exclude profit, but instead considers it a means for achieving human and social ends. Whether such companies distribute dividends or not . . . becomes secondary in relation to their willingness to view profit as a means of achieving the goal of a more humane market and society. It is to be hoped that these new kinds of enterprise will succeed in finding a suitable juridical and fiscal structure in every country. (*CV*, 46)

The challenge for business educators is to understand and explain—even in secular language—the real potential for quite diverse business structures in today's globalized economy.

Chapter 11

Conclusion: *Caritas in veritate* in the Tradition of Catholic Social Thought

PETER KODWO TURKSON

Caritas in veritate is a social encyclical in the tradition of Pope Leo XIII's *Rerum Novarum* (1891).[1] In it the insights of theology, philosophy, economics, ecology, and politics have been harnessed coherently to formulate a social teaching that places total and integral development of the human person at the center of all world systems of thought and activity. The salvation of the human person was at the center of the mission and ministry of Jesus Christ: as the revelation of the love of the Father (John 3:16) and the truth of man's creation in God's image and of his transcendent vocation to holiness and to happiness with God. This is the setting of the two concepts, love and truth, that animate the encyclical. Love and truth do not only lie at the heart of the mission and ministry of Jesus, they also describe the essential character of the life of the human person on earth: originating as a gift and an expression of the love of God and destined to become a gift in love as well.

A true understating of the nature of the Church's social doctrine starts with the faith experience of the ecclesial community itself. Following their response to God's revelation of his love and truth in Jesus, people are transformed and resocialized by the power of God's word and love. This new social reality, the ecclesial community, announces the love and truth of the Trinitarian life that surrounds it

(*CV*, 54). From this experience, people become subjects of love and of truth, agents of a new freedom and a new way of thinking, called to become instruments of grace and communion, spreading the Good News of God's love, weaving networks of love and truth (*CV*, 5). This baptismal experience of life of the ecclesial community does not close in on itself, but interacts at every level with the world. It is in living in Jesus, the Supreme Truth and Good, that the faithful discover anew an appropriate order of goods and an authentic scale of values.

In specifying this role of love and truth in human development, the encyclical may appear to be idealistic, but "this is a method the social teachings of the Church constantly follow, namely, to take the high road, not to distance us from reality, but to draw our attention to the essential point. It is then up to each individual, in a particular country, in a particular profession, in their personal life, to follow through with concrete practice."[2] This dynamic of charity received and given is what gives rise to the Church's social teaching, as in *Caritas in veritate* (*CV*, 5).

Human society, the focus of the Church's social teaching, has changed over the years: from the misery of workers in the days after the Industrial Revolution and the emergence of Marxism (Pope Leo XIII), the Great Depression of 1929 (Pope Pius XI), decolonization and independence of new nations (Pope John XXIII and Pope Paul VI), and the fall of the Berlin Wall and political changes in Eastern Europe (Pope John Paul II) to globalization, underdevelopment, and financial, economic, moral, and anthropological crisis (Pope Benedict XVI, *CV*, 75). In these changing situations, the social encyclicals of the popes have fulfilled the need to embody the basic principles of the Church's social teaching. "The Church's social doctrine illuminates with an unchanging light the new problems that are constantly emerging" (*CV*, 8, 9). The Church's social doctrine in *Caritas in veritate* shines light on the social, global, economic, entrepreneurial, political, anthropological, and ecological problems of our world.

In view of the financial crisis, however, let us quickly note that *Caritas in veritate* is not an economic policy paper with the primary intention of advocating some particular institutional program. In fact, the pope goes to great lengths to stress from the beginning that its central concern is not simply economic development but integral human development or the understanding of true human progress as a vocation.

For Benedict, a proper understanding of the challenges to our moral development requires further and deeper reflection on the economy and its goals, to be sure, but this is only a first step toward bringing about a "profound cultural renewal" that cannot fully be captured by the technical language or categories of academic economics (*CV*, 42).

For Pope Benedict, the phenomenon of globalization, with its positive and negative consequences, is not the result of blind and impersonal historical forces, but rather the organic outgrowth of our deep longing for spiritual unity (*CV*, 18). While the family, and by extension the local community, are the most natural stages for moral flourishing, we are "constitutionally oriented towards 'being more'" (*CV*, 14), always striving to better reflect the image of God in which we are made. This basic inclination toward transcendence expresses itself in the technological inventiveness of our freedom as well as in our ceaseless attempts to conquer and control the forces of nature by our own efforts. And yet, as the Holy Father points out, the "cultural and moral crisis of man" comes about by our "idealizing" either economic or technological progress as the ultimate human goal and leads to a detachment of our goals from moral evaluation and responsibility. Both of these idealizations produce the intoxicating sensation of our own self-sufficient "autonomy" and a misguided notion of "absolute freedom." Our gravitational push toward "being more" should never be confused with the possibility of "being anything" or having everything.

Catholic reflection upon what it means to be authentically human in history and culture goes back to the Fathers of the Church in the second and third centuries. "Throughout the course of history . . . the Church has never failed, in the words of Pope Leo XIII, to speak the words that are hers with regard to questions concerning life in society."[3] However, the Good News of salvation, love, justice, and peace proclaimed by Jesus Christ is not readily received in today's world, which is devastated by war, poverty, and injustice. For this very reason, people everywhere have a greater need than ever of the gospel: of the faith that saves, of the hope that enlightens, of the charity that loves. When the bishops of Africa gathered in synod in October 2009, they expressed the same need of their continent for Christ, saying: "We are therefore committed to pursuing vigorously the proclamation of the Gospel to the people of

Africa, for 'life in Christ is the first and principal factor of development,' as Pope Benedict XVI says in *Caritas in veritate* (CV, 8). "A commitment to development comes from a change of heart, and a change of heart comes from conversion to the Gospel."[4]

It has often been said that the Church is an expert in humanity, and the Church's expertise is rooted in its active engagement in human affairs, ceaselessly looking toward the "new heavens" and "new earth" (2 Pet. 3:13), which she points out in order to help people live their lives in the dimension of authentic meaning. *Gloria Dei vivens homo*: The glory of God is man and woman alive! This sentiment is the reason why the Church teaches not only Catholics but people of goodwill everywhere about the things that truly matter in life.

> Testimony to Christ's charity, through works of justice, peace and development, is part and parcel of evangelization, because Jesus Christ, who loves us, is concerned with the whole person. These important teachings form the basis for the missionary aspect of the Church's social doctrine, which is an essential element of evangelization. The Church's social doctrine proclaims and bears witness to faith. It is an instrument and an indispensable setting for formation in faith. (*CV*, 15)

In the context of faith, the social doctrine of the Church is an instrument of evangelization, because it places the human person and society in relationship to the gospel of Jesus Christ.[5] In short, Catholic social teaching offers a sound approach to thinking about economic and financial realities based on fundamental moral and spiritual principles that speak to the truth of the human person and the centrality of the human family in world affairs.[6]

In the final analysis, the fundamental question concerns the ultimate goals of humanity and the fact that man, with his activity, should build an earthly city that is an anticipation of the heavenly city (*CV*, 7). This outlook should animate the concerns of governments and businesses, nongovernmental organizations, and individuals alike. Faced with the choices involved in finance and economics at every level, there can be no purely financial or economic response. We must look higher.

If, in the end, our goal is to reach "the integral development of man and of all men," according to Popes Paul VI, John Paul II, and now Benedict XVI, the response to these challenges from a Christian standpoint must go beyond the simple question of management, however efficient this may be. Since social relations also have a spiritual dimension, the true response must be both moral and spiritual. It must pass through a conversion implying renewed fidelity to the gospel and an unshakable determination to do nothing that could undermine the divine calling of humanity.

NOTES

Introduction

1. Benedict XVI, homily given at vespers with university students and teachers, St. Peter's Basilica, December 16, 2010. Available at http://www.vatican.va/holy_father/benedict_xvi/homilies/2010/documents/hf_ben-xvi_hom_20101216_vespri-universitari_en.html
2. Pontifical Council for Justice and Peace, Statement on the Origins of the Council, http://www.vatican.va/roman_curia/pontifical_councils/justpeace/documents/rc_pc_justpeace_pro_20011004_en.html.

Chapter 1

1. Bernard Laurent, "Caritas in Veritate as a Social Encyclical: A Modest Challenge to Economic, Social, and Political Institutions," *Theological Studies* 71, no. 3 (September 2010): 515–44.
2. Drew Christiansen, SJ, "Metaphysics and Society: A Commentary on Caritas in Veritate," *Theological Studies* 71, no. 1 (March 2010): 28.
3. J. Hector St. Jean de Crèvecoeur, *Letters from an American Farmer, 1782* (Carlisle, MA: Applewood Books, 2007), Letter III, 56–57.
4. "The Declaration of Independence," July 4, 1776.
5. Crèvecoeur, *Letters*, 49–50. The author was obviously not speaking for the contemporaneous experience of Africans held in the bonds of slavery; nor did he comment on the fact that much of the occupied farmland had previously provided sustenance for Native American tribes.

6. Alexis de Tocqueville, *Democracy in America*, vol. 2, part II, chapter 2 ("On Individualism in Democratic Countries"), trans. Arthur Goldhammer (Whitefish, MT: Kessinger, 2010, 585.
7. Robert Bellah, Richard Madsen, William Sullivan, Ann Swidler, and Steven M. Tipton, *Habits of the Heart: Individualism and Commitment in American Life* (Berkeley: University of California Press, 2008), 275.
8. Ibid., 23.
9. For example, in 1620 as the Massachusetts Bay colonists disembarked from the *Mayflower*, the minister John Winthrop delivered a sermon that conveyed a deep sense of how economic activities and concerns might be permeated by a spirit of mutual interdependence: "We must entertain each other in brotherly affection, we must be willing to abridge ourselves of our superfluities, for the supply of others' necessities. . . . We must delight in each other, make others' conditions our own, rejoice together, mourn together, labour and suffer together, always having before our eyes . . . our community as members of the same body." John Winthrop, "Model of Christian Charity," in *Classics of American Political and Constitutional Thought*, vol. 1, ed. Scott J. Hammond, Kevin R. Hardwick, and Howard L. Lubert (Indianapolis: Hackett, 2007), 17–18. Closer to our own time, it would be enough to think of how Dr. Martin Luther King's religiously grounded description of the "beloved community" caught the imagination of the country and helped to spur positive social change. See, e.g., speech delivered on June 4, 1957, "The Power of Nonviolence," in *A Testament of Hope: The Essential Writings and Speeches of Martin Luther King, Jr.* (San Francisco: Harper, 1991), 12.
10. U.S. Bureau of Economic Analysis, "National Income and Products Accounts: Gross Domestic Product," released 8/27/10.
11. U.S. Bureau of Labor Statistics, "Employment Situation Summary," released November 5, 2010.
12. Christopher Freeman and Carlota Perez, "Structural Crises of Adjustment, Business Cycles and Investment Behaviour," in *Technical Change and Economic Theory*, ed. Giovanni Dosi, Christopher Freeman, Richard Nelson, Gerald Silverberg, and Luc Soete (London: Pinter, 1988); Manuel Castells, *The Rise of the Network Society*, The Information Age: Economy, Society and Culture, vol. 1 (Malden, MA: Blackwell, 1996); Albino Barrera, *Globalization and Economic Ethics: Distributive Justice in the Knowledge Economy* (New York: Palgrave Macmillan, 2007).
13. Albino Barrera, "Globalization's Shifting Economic and Moral Terrain: Contesting Marketplace Mores," *Theological Studies* 69, no. 2 (2009): 290–308.

Chapter 2

1. Joseph Ratzinger, *Introduction to Christology* (San Francisco: Ignatius Press, 2004), 110.

2. Joseph Ratzinger, "Naturrecht, Evangelium und Idologie in der Katholischen Soziallehre" in *Christlicher Glaube und Ideolgie,* ed. Klaus von Bismark and Walter Dirks (Mainz: Grünewald, 1964), 28.
3. In a discussion in Munich with Jurgen Habermas; cf. Joseph Ratzinger, *Werte in Zeiten des Umbruchs: Die Herausforderungen der Zukunft Bestehen* (Frieburg im Breisgau: Herder, 2005), 35.
4. For some ways revelation informed classic Catholic notions of natural law, see Jean Porter, *Natural and Divine Law: Reclaiming the Tradition for Christian Ethics* (Grand Rapids, MI: Eerdmans, 1999). Porter does argue that something like an overlapping consensus can emerge from differing accounts of "the *Humanum.*" See also Mark Murphy, *Natural Law and Practical Rationality* (London: Cambridge University Press, 2002).
5. Lisa Sowell Cahill, "*Caritas in veritate*: Benedict's Global Reorientation," *Theological Studies* 71, no. 2 (June 2010): 302.
6. Thomas Reese, "Pope Benedict on Economic Justice," *Newsweek Blog,* July 2009, where Reese claims that Benedict is "too heavy on personal responsibility and not heavy enough on social change."
7. Inter alia, Emile Durkheim's rich account, against individualistic social contract theory, of the noncontractual (because communitarian and relational) elements in any contract in his *The Division of Labor* (Glencoe, IL: Free Press, 1950). The anthropologist Marcel Mauss, *The Gift* (Glencoe, IL: Free Press, 1954) also lifts up a theme of a culture of giving and an economy based on gift giving.
8. Gary A. Anderson, *Sin: A History* (New Haven, CT: Yale, 2009), 111–32; also 153–60.
9. Ibid., 155.
10. Ibid., 156.
11. See ibid., 161.
12. See ibid., 187.
13. See Clement of Alexandria, "Who Is the Rich Man That Would Be Saved?" in *Clement of Alexandria: With an English Translation,* ed. and trans G. W. Butterworth (London: W. Heinemann, 1919), 32. Quoted in Anderson, *Sin,* 153.
14. See Anderson, *Sin,* 187.
15. See Stefano Zamagni, "Humanizing the Economy: On the Relationship Between the Ethics of Human Rights and Economic Discourse," in *Ethics and the Future of Capitalism,* ed. László Zsolnai and Wojciech Gasparski (New Brunswick, NJ: Transaction, 2002).
16. Pope John Paul II, *Laborem exercens,* (Washington, D.C.: U.S. Catholic Conference, 1981), 12.
17. See also the comment about unemployment and poverty in *CV,* 63.
18. Gene Outka, *Agape: An Ethical Analysis* (New Haven, CT: Yale University Press, 1972), 21–24. For the following analysis see also Outka's chapters 1, 3, and 8, passim.

19. Ignacio Ellacuria, "Discernir el signo de los tiempos," *Diakonia* 17 (1981): 58, as cited in Jon Sobrino, *Where Is God? Earthquake, Terrorism, Barbarity, and Hope,* trans. Margaret Wilde (New York: Orbis, 2004), 51. This interpretation is the opposite of the suggestion by M. Novak that multinational corporations represent the face of the suffering servant in the world.
20. Rolando A. Tuazon, "Narrating Christian Ethics from the Margins: Interdisciplinary and Liberative Ethical Approach to Narratives," *Hapag* 4 (2007), 1–2, 59.
21. I have explained the shift from justice to love in Catholic social teaching in Johan Verstraeten, "Justice Subordinated to Love? The Changing Agenda of Catholic Social Teaching since *Populorum progressio*," in *Responsibility, God and Society: Theological Ethics in Dialogue*, ed. Johan De Tavernier, Jo Selling, Johan Verstraeten, and Paul Schotsmans, Festschrift Roger Burggraeve (Leuven: Peeters/University Press, 2008), 389–405.
22. Synod of Catholic Bishops, *Justice in the World* (1971), section 6. Misunderstandings about these words have led to a reinterpretation of action for justice in terms of "profound links" in *Evangelii Nuntiandi.* The misunderstanding was, however, caused not by the original text but by its translation in German and Dutch, in which *constitutive* was interpreted as "essential."

Chapter 3

1. I expand on this idea of governance through forms other than international governmental organizations in John Coleman, "Global Governance, the State and Multinational Corporations," in *Globalization and Catholic Social Thought: Present Crisis, Future Hope*, ed. John A. Coleman and William Ryan (Maryknoll, NY: Orbis Books, 2005), 239–48. See also Wolfgang Reinecke, *Global Public Policy: Governing Without Government* (Washington, DC: Brookings Institute, 1998); Margaret Keck and Katheryn Sikkink, *Activists Beyond Borders* (Ithaca, NY: Cornell University Press, 1998); and Ann Marie Slaughter, *A New World Order* (Princeton, NJ: Princeton University Press, 2004).

Chapter 4

1. Pontifical Council for Justice and Peace, *Compendium of the Social Doctrine of the Church* (Rome: Libreria Editrice Vaticana, 2004), 33.
2. The Thomistic philosophical and theological underpinnings of this encyclical are evident throughout the text. The clearest example is perhaps St. Thomas Aquinas's argument, "Fides praesupponit cognitionem naturam, sicut gratia naturam et perfectio perfectibile" (*ST* 1 q.2 a.2 ad.1). For Aquinas,

grace perfects human nature, and this perfection is analogous to the relation that exists between the exercise of human will and love. Thus Aquinas writes: "Cum enim gratia non tollat naturam, sed perficiat, oportet quod naturalem ratio subserviat fidei; sicut et naturaliter inclinatio voluntatis obsequiatur caritatis" (*ST* 1 q.1 a.8 ad.2). The encyclical echoes these Thomistic arguments in multiple ways (e.g., relating faith and reason, charity and reason, revelation and human nature, Trinity and society).

3. See John D. Zizioulas, *Communion and Otherness: Further Studies in Personhood and the Church* (New York: T & T Clark, 2006), esp. 13–98; W. Norris Clarke, *The One and the Many: A Contemporary Thomistic Metaphysics* (Notre Dame, IN: University of Notre Dame Press, 2001); Catherine M. LaCugna, *God for Us: The Trinity and Christian Life* (New York: HarperCollins, 1991), esp. 243–317. Note that these contemporary personalist philosophical and theological approaches are not confined to Judeo-Christian circles. For Muslim reflections that presuppose this perspective, see Thomas F. Michel, *A Christian View of Islam: Essay on Dialogue* (Maryknoll, NY: Orbis Books, 2010), esp. 9–49; Miroslav Volf, Ghazi bin Muhammad, and Melissa Yarrington, *A Common Word: Muslims and Christians on Loving God and Neighbor* (Grand Rapids, MI: Eerdmans, 2010).
4. For a discussion of how *Caritas* applies metaphysics to social questions, see Drew Christiansen, "Metaphysics and Society: A Commentary on *Caritas in veritate*," *Theological Studies* 71 (March 2010): 3–28.
5. Robert Bellah, Richard Madsen, William Sullivan, Ann Swidler, and Steven M. Tipton, *Habits of the Heart: Individualism and Commitment in American Life* (Berkeley: University of California Press, 2008), 143.
6. Alexis de Tocqueville, *Democracy in America*, vol. 2, trans. Arthur Goldhammer (Whitefish, MT: Kessinger, 2010), part II, chapter 9 ("How Americans Apply the Doctrine of Self-Interest Rightly Understood in the Matter of Religion"), discussed in Bellah et al., *Habits of the Heart*, 223.
7. Charles Taylor, *Sources of the Self* (Cambridge: Cambridge University Press, 1989), 509–10.
8. Bellah et al., *Habits of the Heart*, 143.
9. Taylor, *Sources of the Self*, 509–10.
10. The flip side—the consequences of the failure to live an authentic life of relationship—can also be a source of inspiration to push toward a redefinition of freedom. See Pope John Paul II, *Centesimus annus*, 41 ("When man does not recognize in himself and in others the value and grandeur of the human person, he effectively deprives himself of the possibility of benefiting from his humanity and of entering into that relationship of solidarity and communion with others for which God created him. Indeed, it is through the free gift of self that man truly finds himself"). See also *Centesimus annus*, 58, describing the preferential option for the poor as an "opportunity": "Justice will never be fully attained unless people see in the poor person, who is asking for help in

order to survive, not an annoyance or a burden, but an opportunity for showing kindness and a chance for greater enrichment. Only such an awareness can give the courage needed to face the risk and the change involved in every authentic attempt to come to the aid of another."

11. Stefano Zamagni, *L'economia del bene comune*, 2nd ed. (Rome: Città Nuova, 2008), 208–9. "No human society can last long, or be a source of happiness or human fulfillment if everyone gives (in an altruistic or philanthropic way), or if everyone demands or expects to receive (either because of opportunism or because of chronic assistance. . .)." See also interview, "Zamagni: diciotto anni dopo la Chiesa non gioca in difesa ma va all'attaco," Ilsussidiario.net (July 8, 2009) (describing the characteristic of the common good "is not sacrifice, but the harmony of respective interests: I need to think of my own interests, but not in a way which are against yours").
12. Stefano Zamagni, "Reciprocity, Civil Economy, Common Good," in *Pursuing the Common Good*, ed. P. Donati and M. Archer (Vatican City: Pontifical Academy of Social Sciences, 2008), 467–502, at xx.
13. Ibid.
14. Zamagni, *L'economia del bene comune*, 209. See also Luigino Bruni, *Reciprocity, Altruism, and the Civil Society* (New York: Routledge, 2008), which explores the extent to which "civil reciprocity" or "'positive' relationality" translates into cooperation.
15. I develop this idea more fully in Mary L. Hirschfeld, "Methodological Stance and Consumption Theory: A Lesson in Feminist Methodology," *History of Political Economy* 29, supplement (1997): 191–211.

Chapter 5

1. One very helpful source for understanding the potential role of reciprocity in economic life is Luigino Bruni and Stefano Zamagni, *Civil Economy: Efficiency, Equity, Public Happiness* (Oxford: Peter Lang, 2007).
2. See, for example, Peter Winch's critique of the importation of the methods and assumptions of physical science into social science in *The Idea of Social Science and Its Relation to Philosophy*, 2nd ed. (New York: Routledge, 1990).
3. See, for example, Clifford Geertz, *The Interpretation of Cultures* (London: Hutchinson Press, 1975).
4. Josef Pieper, *An Anthology* (San Francisco: Ignatius Press, 1989), 138. See also Josef Pieper, *Leisure: The Basis of Culture* (South Bend, IN: St. Augustine's Press, 1998), 19.
5. Pieper, *An Anthology*, 139. See also Jacques Godbout's discussion of the premises of Alcoholics Anonymous, namely that the alcoholic "cannot solve his or her problem alone, and must recognize that the capacity to find a solution

comes from outside, from a gift bestowed by a superior force." *The World of the Gift* (Montreal: McGill-Queen's University Press, 1998), 69.

6. See Pieper, *Leisure*, chapter 2. Pieper sees this inability to receive as both an ethical and epistemological problem. He explains that Kant's notion of knowledge work plays a destructive role in this significant problem of not receiving.
7. Karl Rahner, "Theological Remarks on the Problem of Leisure," in *Theological Investigation*, vol. 1, trans. Kevin Smyth (Baltimore: Helican Press, 1966), 379.
8. Joseph Ratzinger, *Introduction to Christianity*, trans. J. R. Foster (San Francisco: Ignatius Press, 1990), 266.
9. David Schindler, "Christology and the Imago Dei: Interpreting Gaudium et spes," *Communio* 23 (Spring 1996): 159.
10. Ratzinger, *Introduction to Christianity*, 266. See also *Caritas in veritate*, 52.
11. *Caritas in veritate*, 34, 37. "Space also needs to be created within the market for economic activity carried out by subjects who freely choose to act according to principles other than those of pure profit, without sacrificing the production of economic value in the process. The many economic entities that draw their origin from religious and lay initiatives demonstrate that this is concretely possible" (37). See for example the companies associated with the Economy of Communion, family businesses, cooperatives, entrepreneurial ventures, other types of firms inspired by faith, etc. These communities of persons are not without their contracts and economic rationality, but these realities do not exhaust the meaning of such communities.

Chapter 6

1. L. Bouckaert, "Spirituality and Economic Democracy: A Personalist Approach," in *Spirituality and Ethics in Management*, ed. L. Zsolnai (Amsterdam: Kluwer, 2004), 51–58; L. Bouckaert, "From Business Ethics to Business Spirituality: The Socratic Model of Leadership," in *Spirituality and Business: Exploring Possibilities for a New Management Paradigm*, ed. S. Nandram and M. E. Borden (Heidelberg: Springer, 2010), 73–87.
2. Otto Scharmer, *Theory U: Leading from the Future as It Emerges* (Cambridge, MA: Society for Organizational Learning, 2007).
3. Peter Pruzan and Kirsten Pruzan Mikkelsen, eds., *Leading with Wisdom: Spiritual-Based Leadership in Business* (Sheffield: Greenleaf, 2007).
4. See S. A. Cortright and Michael Naughton, eds., *Rethinking the Purpose of Business* (Notre Dame, IN: University of Notre Dame Press, 2002).
5. Robert K. Greenleaf, *The Institution as Servant* (Westfield, IN: Greenleaf Center for Servant Leadership, 1972).
6. Michael Novak, *Toward a Theology of the Corporation* (Washington, DC: AEI Press, 1990).

7. Gary Hamel, "Moon Shots for Management," *Harvard Business Review* (February 2009): 93.
8. See Jacques Maritain, *The Person and the Common Good* (Notre Dame, IN: University of Notre Dame, 1966), 16. See *Caritas in veritate*, 11, "Without the perspective of eternal life, human progress in this world is denied breathing-space." Once ideas, whether about corporate social responsibility, human rights, business ethics, philanthropy, or social entrepreneurship, are severed from transcendent roots, they are prone to a mechanical repetition that, over time, empties itself of its meaning and importance.
9. This seems to me to be one of Benedict's contributions to the Catholic social tradition—reconnecting us to the theological ground that is the fundamental resource not only to its intellectual understanding but to its affective connection and willful acts. It is a tradition that does not merely add one more level of motivation to economic life, but rather reorders this life to its deepest roots in God's gift of love mediated through vocation, virtues, prayer, discernment, etc.
10. Stephen J. Porth, John J. McCall, and Joseph A. DiAngelo, "Business Education at Catholic Universities: Current Status and Future Directions," *Journal of Catholic Higher Education* 28, no. 1 (Winter 2009): 3–22. Of those schools with undergraduate learning goals, over 80 percent of the respondents "measured student outcomes with respect to ethics education but only 6% assessed learning with respect to religious identity."
11. See James Davidson Hunter, *To Change the World: The Irony, Tragedy, and Possibility of Christianity in the Late Modern World* (New York: Oxford University Press, 2010).
12. Benedict is giving a wide variety of terms in relation to the broad notion of gift: gift, logic of gift, principle of gratuitousness, fraternity, solidarity, spirit of gift, the logic of the unconditional gift, fraternal reciprocity, justice (right relationships), community, mutualist principles, etc. More time and thought will be needed to understand the relationships among these terms.

Chapter 7

1. *Report by the Commission on the Measurement of Economic Performance and Social Progress*, 2009, Executive Summary, para. 1.
2. Economists take it as a fixed postulate that human desire is infinite. Since resources are finite, this means that scarcity can never be escaped. Economics defines itself as the science of scarcity.
3. Economists do have room for altruism, but it involves an opportunity cost. If our desires were satiable, this would not necessarily be the case.
4. It would take too long to develop, but the underlying account of practical reason is really not compatible with the model of utility maximization

employed by economists. It is not merely that we have no reason to think humans are good at doing that sort of maximization, as I argued above. It is that to focus on practical reason as an exercise in calculation is to entirely miss the receptive or contemplative side of reason, which is an essential part of genuine truth seeking.

5. Milton Friedman, *Capitalism and Freedom* (Chicago: University of Chicago Press, 1962), 13.
6. Richard Posner, *The Economics of Justice* (Cambridge, MA: Harvard University Press, 1981), 94.
7. Fabienne Peter, "Choice, Consent and the Legitimacy of Market Transactions," *Economics and Philosophy* 20 (2004): 1–18.

Chapter 8

1. George Weigel, "Caritas in Veritate in Gold and Red," National Review Online, July 7, 2009.
2. Andrea Tornielli and Paolo Rodari, *Attacco a Ratzinger: Accuse e scandali, profezie e complotti contro Benedetto XVI*, (Milano: Piemme 2010), 145.
3. Bill Bishop, *The Big Sort: Why Clustering of Like-Minded America Is Tearing Us Apart* (New York: Houghton Mifflin Harcourt, 2008), 14.
4. United States Catholic Bishops, *Economic Justice for All: Pastoral Letter on Catholic Social Teaching and the U.S. Economy* (Washington, DC: United States Conference of Catholic Bishops, 1986), 135.

Chapter 9

1. Mary L. Hirschfeld, "Objectivity and the Theory of Maximizing Behavior: A Lesson in Feminist Methodology," *History of Political Economy* 29, supplement (1997), 191–211.
2. An example: "In order *to construct* an economy that will soon be in a position to serve the national and global common good" (*CV*, 41, emphasis added).
3. This is also the thesis of Bernard Laurent, "*Caritas in veritate* as a Social Encyclical: A Modest Challenge to Economic, Social and Political Institutions," *Theological Studies* 71 (September 2010): 544.
4. Erik Borgman, *Want de plaats waarop je staat is heilige grond: God als onderzoeksprogramma* (Amsterdam: Boom, 2008), 64.
5. For a more thorough interpretation of scrutinizing the signs of the times, see Johan Verstraeten, "Catholic Social Thought as Discernment," in *Scrutinizing the Signs of the Times in the Light of the Gospel*, ed. Johan Verstraeten (Leuven: Peeters/University Press), 1–16.

6. Erik Borgman, "Metamorfosen. Over religie en moderne cultuur, zoals geciteerd door Christophe Brabant," *Tertio*, September 19, 2007, 14.
7. For a reflection on this problem see Johan de Tavernier, "Eschatology and Social Ethics," in *Personalist Morals: Essays in Honor of Professor Louis Janssens*, ed. Joseph A. Selling (Leuven: Peeters/University Press, 1988), 279–300.
8. Cf. Ronald A. Heifetz, *Leadership Without Easy Answers* (Cambridge, MA: Belknap, 1994), 24.
9. This is also the conclusion of Bernard Laurent, who argues that there is even a "refusal to deliver any form of analysis of the structures" ("*Caritas in veritate* as a Social Encyclical," 538). This is not completely correct since there are in *Caritas in veritate* hints of the structural dimensions of problems, particularly with regard to the poor, as we will see further.
10. Jon Sobrino, *The Principle of Mercy: Taking the Crucified People from the Cross* (Maryknoll, NY: Orbis Books, 1994), 51.
11. I quote with permission from an unpublished paper, "The Common Good as an Ethical Framework for Development," presented by Anthonette Mendoza at the first social week in the UK organized by Las Casas Institute for Ethics, Governance and Social Justice, 2010, 5.

Chapter 10

1. Clay Shirky, *Cognitive Surplus* (New York: Penguin, 2010), location 147–61 in the Kindle version.
2. Milton Friedman, "The Social Responsibility of Business Is to Increase Its Profits," *New York Times Magazine*, September 13, 1970, 32, 33.
3. Stephen G. Gilles, "The Invisible Hand Formula," *Virginia Law Review* 80 (1994): 1015, 1048.
4. For a more extensive discussion of this application, see Amelia J. Uelmen, "Toward a Trinitarian Theory of Products Liability," *Journal of Catholic Social Thought* 1 (2004): 603–45.
5. A convincing argument for this thesis can be found in Austen Ivereigh, *Faithful Citizens: A Practical Guide to Catholic Social Teaching and Community Organising* (London: Darton, Longman and Todd, 2010).
6. According to Hannah Arendt, *The Human Condition*, 2nd ed. (Chicago: University of Chicago Press, 1998), 175–247, the human person is not only an "animal laborans," nor a "homo faber" but first of all a person who realises himself or herself through human action, and that necessarily includes political participation. She also suggests, for example, that the main contribution of trade unions is not in the economic sphere but in the political: ended to the exclusion of workers from the political decision-making process.

7. Ivereigh, *Faithful Citizens*, 169.
8. Pontifical Council for Justice and Peace, *Compendium of the Social Doctrine of the Church* (Rome: Libreria Editrice Vaticana, 2004), 189.
9. Ivereigh, *Faithful Citizens*, 52. He articulates his vision on participation in more detail in chapter 4, 70–89.
10. Ibid., 51.
11. Jonathan Sacks, *Education Values and Religion* (St. Andrews: University of St. Andrews, 1996), as quoted by Ivereigh, *Faithful Citizens*, 51.
12. Ivereigh, *Faithful Citizens*, 51.
13. Ibid., 52.
14. W. Van De Donk, *De gedragen gemeenschap. Over katholiek maatschappelijk organiseren de ontzuiling voorbij* (The Hague: SdU Uitgevers, 2001).
15. Michael Walzer, "Introduction," in *Toward a Global Civil Society*, ed. Michael Walzer (Providence, RI: Berghahn Books, 1995), 3.
16. Amartya Sen, *The Idea of Justice* (London: Allen Lane/Penguin, 2009), xii.
17. Dean Maines and Michael Naughton, "Middle Level Thinking: The Importance of Connecting and Mediating Catholic Social Thought, Corporate Social Responsibility, And Business Practice," position paper, 6th International Symposium on Catholic Social Thought and Management Education, October 5–7, 2006, Pontifical University of St. Thomas (Angelicum), Rome, 2, http://www.stthomas.edu/cathstudies/cst/conferences/thegoodcompany/Papers/00POSITION%20Paper%20MLT.pdf.

Chapter 11

1. Counting the letter of the Sacred Congregation of the Council to Mons. Liénart, Bishop of Lille, on June 5, 1929, two documents of Vatican Council II (*Gaudium et spes* and "Dignitatis Humane"), the second half of the encyclical letter *Deus caritas est*, and the instruction *Dignitas Personae, on Certain Bioethical Questions* from the Congregation for the Doctrine of the Faith (December 8, 2009), one may reckon with twenty-two official documents on the social teaching of the church. Cf. *Le Discours social de l'Église Catholique: De Léon XIII à Benoit XVI* (Paris: Bayard Montrouge, 2009).
2. "C'est une method constant de la doctrine social de l'Eglise: prendre dela hauteur, non pour nous èloigner de reel mais pour nous rapprocher de l'essential. Ensuite a chacun, dans son pays, dans son métier, dans sa vie personnelle, d'en tirer les consequences practiques." J.-Y. Naudet, "Caritas in veritate. La Doctrine sociale de l'Eglise: un unique enseignement," *Annales de Vendèe* no. 5 (2009): 140.
3. Cardinal Renato Martino, "Introductory Letter," in *Compendium of the Social Doctrine of the Church*, by Pontifical Council for Justice and Peace (Rome: Libreria Editrice Vaticana, 2004).

4. Special Assembly of Bishops for Africa, "Message to the People of God," October 23, 2009, para. 15.
5. Cf. Pontifical Council for Justice and Peace, *Compendium*, xx–xxv.
6. Fr. Gianpaolo Salvini, SJ, prefers to describe these striking features of the encyclical as "Le novità dell' enciclica." See Gianpaolo Salvini, "l'Encicilica 'Caritas in Veritate,'" *La Civiltà Cattolica*, no. 3822 (September 19, 2009), 469–70. The ideas expressed here are taken from him.

BIBLIOGRAPHY

Anderson, Gary A. *Sin: A History*. New Haven, CT: Yale University Press, 2009.

Arendt, Hannah. *The Human Condition*. Chicago: University of Chicago Press, 1998.

Barrera, Albino. *Globalization and Economic Ethics: Distributive Justice in the Knowledge Economy*. New York: Palgrave Macmillan, 2007.

———. "Globalization's Shifting Economic and Moral Terrain: Contesting Marketplace Mores." *Theological Studies* 69, no. 2 (2009): 290–308.

Bellah, Robert, Richard Madsen, William Sullivan, Ann Swidler, and Steven M. Tipton. *Habits of the Heart: Individualism and Commitment in American Life* (1985). Berkeley: University of California Press, 2008.

Benedict XVI. *Caritas in veritate*, Origins (Jul 16 2009), 39(9): 129–159.

Bishop, Bill. *The Big Sort: Why Clustering of Like-Minded America Is Tearing Us Apart*. New York: Houghton Mifflin Harcourt, 2008.

Borgman, Erik. "Metamorfosen. Over religie en moderne cultuur, zoals geciteerd door Christophe Brabant." *Tertio* 19 (September 2007): 14.

———. *Want de plaats waarop je staat is heilige grond: God als onderzoeksprogramma*. Amsterdam: Boom, 2008.

Bouckaert, L. "From Business Ethics to Business Spirituality: The Socratic Model of Leadership." In *Spirituality and Business: Exploring Possibilities for a New Management Paradigm*. Edited by S. Nandram and M. E. Borden. Heidelberg: Springer, 2010.

———. "Spirituality and Economics Democracy: A Personalist Approach." In *Spirituality and Ethics in Management*. Edited by L. Zsolnai. Amsterdam: Kluwer, 2004.

Bruni, Luigino. *Reciprocity, Altruism, and the Civil Society*. New York: Routledge, 2009.

Bruni, Luigino, and Stefano Zamagni. *Civil Economy: Efficiency, Equity, Public Happiness.* Oxford: Peter Lang, 2007.

Cahill, Lisa Sowell. "Caritas in veritate: Benedict's Global Reorientation." *Theological Studies* 72 (June 2010): 302.

Castells, Manuel. *The Rise of the Network Society.* The Information Age: Economy, Society and Culture, Volume 1. Malden, MA: Blackwell, 1996.

Christiansen, Drew, SJ. "Metaphysics and Society: A Commentary on Caritas in Veritate." *Theological Studies* 71, no. 1 (March 2010): 3–28.

Clark, W. Norris. *The One and the Many: A Contemporary Thomistic Metaphysics.* Notre Dame, IN: University of Notre Dame Press, 2001.

Clement of Alexandria. "Who Is the Rich Man That Would Be Saved?" In *Clement of Alexandria: With an English Translation.* Edited and translated by G. W. Butterworth. London: W. Heinemann, 1919.

Coleman, John A., SJ. "Global Governance, the State and Multinational Corporations." In *Globalization and Catholic Social Thought: Present Crisis, Future Hope.* Edited by John A. Coleman, SJ, and William Ryan, SJ. Maryknoll, NY: Orbis Books, 2005.

Crèvecoeur, J. Hector St. Jean de. *Letters from an American Farmer, 1782.* Carlisle, MA: Applewood Books, 2007.

de Tavernier, Johan. "Eschatology and Social Ethics." *Personlist Morals: Essays in Honor of Professor Louis Janssens.* Edited by Joseph A. Selling. Leuven: Peeters/University Press, 1988.

de Tavernier, Johan, Jo Selling, Johan Verstraeten, and Paul Schotsmans, eds. *Responsibility, God and Society: Theological Ethics in Dialogue.* Leuven: Peeters/University Press, 2008.

Durkheim, Emile. *The Division of Labor.* Glencoe, IL: Free Press, 1950.

Ella, Ignacio. "Discernir el signo de los tiempos." *Diakonia* 17 (1981): 58.

Freeman, Christopher, and Carlota Perez. "Structural Crises of Adjustment, Business Cycles and Investment Behavior." In *Technical Change and Economic Theory.* Edited by Giovannie Dosi, Christoper Freeman, Richard Nelson, Gerald Silverberg, and Luc Soete. London: Pinter, 1988.

Friedman, Milton. *Capitalism and Freedom.* Chicago: University of Chicago Press, 1962.

———. "The Social Responsibility of Business Is to Increase Its Profits. *New York Times Magazine,* September 13, 1970, 32, 33.

Geertz, Clifford. *The Interpretation of Cultures.* London: Hutchinson Press, 1975.

Gilles, Stephen G. "The Invisible Hand Formula." *Virginia Law Review* 80 (1994): 1015, 1048.

Godbout, Jacques. *The World of the Gift.* Montreal: McGill-Queen's University Press, 1998.

Greenleaf, Robert K. *The Institution as Servant.* Westfield, IN: Greenleaf Center for Servant Leadership, 1972.

Hamel, Gary. "Moon Shots for Management." *Harvard Business Review* (February 2009): 93.

Hammond, Scott J., Kevin R. Hardwick, and Howard L. Lubert. *Classics of American Political and Constitutional Thought*, Volume 1. Indianapolis: Hackett, 2007.

Heifetz, Ronald A. *Leadership Without Easy Answers*. Cambridge, MA: Belknap, 1994.

Hirschfeld, Mary L. "Methodological Stance and Consumption Theory: A Lesson in Feminist Methodology." *History of Political Economy* 29, supplement (1997): 191–211.

Hunter, James Davidson. *To Change the World: The Irony, Tragedy, and Possibility of Christianity in the Late Modern World*. New York: Oxford University Press, 2010.

Ivereigh, Austen. *Faithful Citizens: A Practical Guide to Catholic Social Teaching and Community Organising*. London: Darton, Longman and Todd, 2010.

Keck, Margaret, and Katheryn Sikknilk. *Activists Beyond Borders*. Ithaca, NY: Cornell University Press, 2004.

King, Martin Luther. *A Testament of Hope: The Essential Writings and Speeches of Martin Luther King, Jr.* San Francisco: Harper, 1991.

LaCugna, Catherine M. *God for Us: The Trinity and Christian Life*. New York: Harper Collins, 1991.

Laurent, Bernard. "*Caritas in veritate* as a Social Encyclical: A Modest Challenge to Economic, Social and Political Institutions." *Theological Studies* 71 (September 2010): 515–44.

Maritain, Jacques. *The Person and the Common Good*. Notre Dame, IN: University of Notre Dame Press, 1966.

Mauss, Marcel. *The Gift*. Glencoe, IL: Free Press, 1954.

Michel, Thomas F. *A Christian View of Islam: Essay on Dialogue*. Maryknoll, NY: Orbis Books, 2010.

Murphy, Mark. *Natural Law and Practical Rationality*. London: Cambridge University Press, 2002.

Novak, Michael. *Toward a Theology of the Corporation*. Washington, DC: AEI Press, 1990.

Outka, Gene. *Agape: An Ethical Analysis*. New Haven, CT: Yale University Press, 1972.

Peter, Fabienne. "Choice, Consent and the Legitimacy of Market Transactions." *Economics and Philosophy* 20 (2004): 1–18.

Pieper, Josef. *An Anthology*. San Francisco: Ignatius Press, 1989.

———. *Leisure: The Basics of Culture*. South Bend, IN: St. Augustine's Press, 1998.

Pontifical Council for Justice and Peace. *Compendium of the Social Doctrine of the Church*. Rome: Libreria Editrice Vaticana, 2004.

Porter, Jean. *Natural and Divine Law: Reclaiming the Tradition for Christian Ethics.* Grand Rapids, MI: Eerdmans, 1999.

Porth, Stephen J., John J. McCall, and Joseph A. DiAngelo. "Business Education at Catholic Universities: Current Status and Future Directions." *Journal of Catholic Higher Education* 28, no. 1 (Winter 2009): 3–22.

Posner, Richard. *The Economics of Justice.* Cambridge, MA: Harvard University Press, 1981.

Pruzan, Peter, and Kristen Mikkelsen, eds. *Rethinking the Purpose of Business.* Notre Dame, IN: University of Notre Dame Press, 2002.

Rahner, Karl. "Theological Remarks on the Problem of Leisure." *Theological Investigations* 1 (1966): 379.

Ratzinger, Joseph. *Introduction to Christology.* San Francisco: Ignatius Press, 2004.

———. "Naturrecht, Evangelium und Idologie in der Katholischen." In *Christlicher Glaube und Ideolgie.* Edited by Klaus von Bismark and Walter Dirks. Mainz: Grünewald, 1964.

———. *Werte in Zeiten des Umbruchs: Die Herausforderungen der Zukunft Bestehen.* Frieburg im Breisgau: Herder, 2005.

Reese, Thomas. "Pope Benedict on Economic Justice." *Newsweek Blog,* July 2009.

Reinecke, Wolfgang. *Global Public Policy: Governing Without Government.* Washington, DC: Brookings Institute, 1998.

Sacks, Jonathan. *Education, Values and Religion.* St. Andrews, UK: University of St. Andrews, 1996.

Salvini, Gianpaolo, SJ. "l'Encicilica 'Caritas in Veritate.'" *La Civiltà Cattolica,* no. 3822 (September 19, 2009): 469–70.

Scharmer, Otto. *Theory U: Leading from the Future as It Emerges.* Cambridge, MA: Society for Organizational Learning, 2007.

Schindler, David. "Christology and the Imago Dei: Interpreting Gaudium et spes." *Communio* 23 (Spring 1966): 159.

Selling, Joseph A. *Personlist Morals: Essays in Honor of Professor Louis Janssens.* Leuven: Peeters/University Press, 1988.

Sen, Amartya. *The Idea of Justice.* London: Allen Lane/Penguin Books, 2009.

Shirky, Clay. *Cognitive Surplus.* New York: Penguin, 2010.

Slaughter, Ann Marie. *A New World Order.* Princeton, NJ: Princeton University Press, 2004.

Sobrino, Jon. *The Principle of Mercy: Taking the Crucified People from the Cross.* Maryknoll, NY: Orbis Books, 1994.

———. *Where Is God? Earthquake, Terrorism, Barbarity and Hope.* Translated by Margaret Wilde. New York: Orbis Books, 2004.

Synod of Catholic Bishops. *Justice in the World.* Vatican City: Typis Polyglottis Vaticanis, 1971.

Taylor, Charles. *Sources of Self.* Cambridge: Cambridge University Press, 1989.

Tocqueville, Alexis de. *Democracy in America,* Volume 2. Translated by Arthur Goldhammer. Whitefish, MT: Kessinger, 2010.

Tuazon, Roland A. "Narrating Christian Ethics from the Margins: Interdisciplinary and Liberative Ethical Approach to Narratives." *Hapag* 4 (2007): 1–2, 59.

Uelmen, Amelia J. "Toward a Trinitarian Theory of Products Liability." *Journal of Catholic Social Thought* 1 (2004): 603–45.

Van De Donk, W. *De gedragen gemeenschap. Over katholiek maatschappelijik organiseren de ontzuiling voorbij.* The Hague: SdU Uitgevers, 2001.

Verstraeten, Johan. "Catholic Social Thought as Discernment." In *Scrutinizing the Signs of the Times in the Light of the Gospel.* Edited by Johan Verstraeten. Leuven: Peeters Leuven University Press, 2007.

———. "Justice Subordinated to Love? The Changing Agenda of Catholic Social Teaching since *Populorum progressio.*" In *Responsibility, God and Society. Theological Ethics in Dialogue.* Edited by Johan De Tavernier, Joseph A. Selling, Johan Verstraeten, and Paul Schotsmans. Leuven: Peeters/University Press, 2008.

Volf, Miroslav, Ghazi Bin Muhammad, and Melissa Yarrington. *A Common Word: Muslims and Christians on Loving God and Neighbor.* Grand Rapids, MI: Eerdmans, 2010.

Walzer, Michael. "Introduction." In *Toward a Global Civil Society.* Edited by Michael Walzer. Providence, RI: Berghahn Books, 1995.

Winch, Peter. *The Idea of Social Science and Its Relation to Philosophy.* 2nd ed. New York: Routledge, 1990.

Zamagni, Stefano. "Humanizing the Economy: On the Relationship Between the Ethics of Human Rights and Economic Discourse." In *Ethics and the Future of Capitalism.* Edited by Lázló Zsolnai and Wojciech Gasparski. New Brunswick, NJ: Transaction, 2002.

———. *L'economia del bene comune.* 2nd ed. Rome: Citta Nuova, 2008.

———. "Reciprocity, Civil Economy, Common Good." In *Pursuing the Common Good.* Edited by P. Donati and M. Archer. Vatican City: Pontifical Academy of Social Sciences, 2008.

Zizioulas, John D. *Communion and Otherness: Further Studies in Personhood and the Church.* New York: T & T Clark, 2006.

Zsolnai, Lázló, and Wojciech Gasparski, eds. *Ethics and the Future of Capitalism.* New Brunswick, NJ: Transaction, 2002.

INDEX